STRONGMAN
MY STORY

Eddie 'The Beast' Hall

1 3 5 7 9 10 8 6 4 2

Virgin Books, an imprint of Ebury Publishing,
20 Vauxhall Bridge Road,
London SW1V 2SA

Virgin Books is part of the Penguin Random House group of companies whose addresses can be found at global.penguinrandomhouse.com

First published by Virgin Books in 2017

www.penguin.co.uk

A CIP catalogue record for this book is available from the British Library

HB ISBN 9780753548707
TPB ISBN 9780753548981

Typeset in India by Integra Software Services Pvt. Ltd, Pondicherry

Printed and bound in Great Britain by Clays Ltd, St Ives PLC

For Nan and Alex

CONTENTS

PROLOGUE

9 July 2016, 7.45 p.m.
World Deadlift Championship, First Direct Arena, Leeds

'Fifteen minutes to go, Eddie.'

'Yeah, all right. Fuck off, will you?'

'Is there anything you need?'

'Yeah, there is: for you to fuck off. Don't worry, dickhead. I'll be ready.'

This is one of the few occasions when swearing doesn't get me into a shit load of trouble. They know what I'm like backstage at a competition and so it's water off a duck's back. I'll still apologise later. It's at the end of the night when the fines start being dished out and it's usually because somebody's been daft enough to stick a microphone in front of me.

'So, Eddie. How do you feel about winning Britain's Strongest Man?'

'Fucking excellent, brother.'

'CUT!'

I've already been in trouble once tonight. A few minutes ago I pulled 465kg (1,025 lb), which, although just a stepping stone to the main event, is still a new world record. After the lift the presenter, Colin Bryce, asked me what I was going to do next. 'Unleash the beast,' was what I meant to say, but when I opened my mouth and started speaking, a word beginning with F found its way into the sentence. The crowd also know what I'm like and they thought it was hilarious.

I don't do it to impress anybody or to piss anybody off. I do it because, rightly or wrongly, it's part of who I am and it's almost impossible for me to deviate from that. There is no 'Eddie Zero', I'm afraid. No low-calorie alternative. I'm full fat, mate, and – much to my mum's regret and embarrassment – another word beginning with F.

In fifteen minutes' time, at precisely 8 p.m., I will pull 500kg (1,102 lb) in front of 10,000 people and in doing so become the first human being in the history of the world to lift half a tonne. Let me say that again, boys and girls: half a tonne. That's about the same weight as an overfed racehorse.

Notice I've left out the words 'attempt to', by the way. The definition of the word attempt is 'to make an effort to achieve', which means there is always a possibility of failure. Not tonight. Not here. This, my friend, is history in the making and ensuring such occurrences take place is the reason I have been put on this earth. Some people are here to build houses and work in banks, and some people are here to change the world.

Being a foul-mouthed history-making cheeky behemoth does come at a cost, however. Ever since agreeing to do the lift I have had to virtually ignore my wife and kids and over the last six months I have spent no more than a few hours in their company. That in itself has obviously been a massive sacrifice for all of us, but in truth it's just the tip of the iceberg. My daily routine has been to eat, sleep, train, recover and repeat, and in addition to a couple of short but extremely severe bouts of depression, which I think were triggered by stress and isolation, I have gradually become less mobile. This is because, in order to lift such a massive weight, I have had to put on an extra 15kg (33 lb) in weight and right now I am just over thirty-one stone. My God, it's been hard though. I have suffered all kinds of pain over the years but preparing for this has been a different kind of hell and even now I am in a very, very dark place.

As I sit quietly in the dressing room I suddenly belch, and am reminded of what I had for my dinner – or lunch, if you're posh. Whilst everyone else will have been tucking into sandwiches or burgers, I was in a restaurant ordering a mouth-watering lump of fat taken straight from a massive joint of gammon. In terms of taste it was probably one of the most disgusting meals I've ever eaten, but in terms of calories, it was the dog's. About 4,000, all told.

You see, to me, when it comes to milestones, the half-tonne deadlift is right up there with the four-minute mile and if anybody ever manages to break the record once I've smashed it – and they will – it will be my record they're breaking. Let's face it, nobody gives a damn who holds the current record for running a mile, and why would they? Whoever holds the record is simply clinging to the coattails of greatness. The only name that matters when it comes to running the mile is Roger Bannister, and why? Because he proved the naysayers wrong and did what everyone said was impossible. He became – and remains – the benchmark and regardless of the fact that the record he set is now slow in comparison to today's athletes, it is the only one we really care about. He walks (or runs) on a higher plane to the rest and in a few minutes' time he'll have to make some room – quite a bit of room, actually – for me.

The reason this is relevant now is because the only person in this entire arena who thinks I'm going to pull this lift is me. Some of my mates probably think I have a chance, but the bookies are offering odds of 25/1 and so have me down as a complete no-hoper. That's fine though. Other people's doubt is my biggest motivation and the fact that the no's are unanimous makes it a forgone conclusion as far as I'm concerned.

'OK, we're ready for you, Eddie.'

'Come on then, fucker, lead the way.'

After a quick detour to a disabled toilet, which I'll explain later, my three-man entourage and I make our way to the stage. As we pass the other athletes one or two of them shout, 'Good luck, Ed,' but I know not one of them thinks I can do it. Seeing them all staring at me is like a last-minute shot of adrenalin.

One man not staring at me from the pool of athletes, but whose words echo through my mind, is four-time World's Strongest Man, Brian Shaw. Brian should be here, but he pulled out of the event announcing that 500kg was ridiculous. In fact, the current World's Strongest Man had publicly proclaimed that 480kg (1,058 lb) was the absolute max he thought was doable by anyone.

As we walk on I over Žydrūnas Savickas – arguably the strongest men in history – voicing his concerns about the feat I'm about to attempt. 'What happens to the human body at such a weight,' he says. 'I am not sure we are designed to handle that amount. It is a little dangerous but we shall see.'

I respect both men but I will make them eat their words.

We're almost at the stage now and I can hear the MC warming up the crowd. This is supposed to be the support event for Europe's Strongest Man but it should be the other way around. Whoever wins that title won't be making history. They won't be on Roger Bannister's higher plane.

As I walk through the curtain onto the stage the first thing I see is the crowd, all 10,000 of them. The biggest audience ever for a strongman event. A hit of smelling salts brings that familiar wild, yet strangely pleasurable pain burning through my skull. I gesture to the crowd to make some noise and they respond with a deafening roar. This, right now, is the deepest, darkest moment of my life.

Over the past twenty years only 9kg (20 lb) has been added to the world deadlift record. What am I going to add? 35kg (77 lb)? Bloody hell.

As I bend down and put the straps around my hands everything goes quiet. I'm locked in now. I am in the zone, as they say. I've visualised this moment a thousand times and I've practiced it a thousand more. Rep after rep of drills, hour after hour of training in the gym has led me to this moment. I'll hear the crowd again once I've locked my back out, but for the next ten seconds or so it's just me and the bar.

As I find my grip, I see, just fleetingly, a picture of my family in my mind's eye. It's a quick but important reminder of exactly why I'm doing this.

I'm happy with the grip now, so am ready to go.

OK, Roger. Shove up a bit, mate. It's time to make some history.

CHAPTER 1

Eight Pounds, Fourteen Ounces

Believe it or not, give or take a pound or two, my weight has always matched my age (or at least it did until I hit twenty-nine stone). So at the time of writing I'm nearly thirty years old and a nice healthy thirty-odd stone. At six foot three inches I'm quite a noticeable presence in a confined space, shall we say.

When they meet me, a lot of people say that they can't imagine me being anything other than big, so these first few chapters are going to be a bit of a revelation to some. It's the same when Mum and Dad get the photograph albums out. Whoever's unlucky enough to be shown them will see one of me as a kid messing about on a beach or something, and then say, 'Naaaa. That can't be Eddie!' It gets on my tits sometimes.

Anyway, you can check this with my mum if you like but at birth, I, Edward Stephen Hall, weighed eight pounds and fourteen ounces exactly, having been born at North Staffs Maternity Hospital to Stephen and Helen Hall at 4.59 p.m.

on Friday 15 January 1988. According to the internet I share a birthday with Martin Luther King Jr and the rapper Pitbull, which actually makes perfect sense: a man who inspired millions and a success story who's named after an angry and potentially dangerous dog. I'll take that. What is perhaps more relevant is the fact that I seem to be the only sportsperson of note to have been born on 15 January 1988. As somebody who doesn't like sharing things – especially titles, world records and podiums – that suits me down to the ground.

According to Mum and Dad I was a very happy and easy-going baby who loved being cuddled; particularly by Mum and her own mum, Nan. Nan was an amazing woman and when I started getting into trouble she was one of the only people who could get through to me. More about that later.

I have two older brothers, Alex and James, and while Mum and Nan wanted to hug me, those two wanted to kill me. I don't think there was any jealousy involved, like there is in some cases. They just saw a fat little shit move into the house and decided they were going to kick his ass.

One of the earliest examples of this reprehensible behaviour happened when I was just a few weeks old. My brother, James, who today plays professional rugby for Bristol yet still weighs a mere eighteen stone, decided to lift me up by my neck and then drop me on the floor, and because he was only about eighteen months old he obviously got away with it. I'd like to see him try that now. In fact, I'd like to see anybody try it. My eldest brother, Alex, who was three when I was born and is now about a foot shorter (ha ha), probably did the same and worse when nobody else was looking and so the fact that I made it to nine months is a miracle.

The reason I mention this particular age is that it heralded my first visit back to a hospital, yet strangely enough it had nothing to do with either of my homicidal siblings. The problem started when I suddenly began sleeping about twenty-three hours a day. Although Mum and Dad must have been relieved by this, it obviously wasn't normal and so I was taken into hospital to have a few tests. The diagnosis was severe anaemia and once they managed to get a bit more iron into me I was fine. Children and babies are especially susceptible to anaemia during periods of rapid growth and so looking back I'm surprised I didn't get it every week.

By the time I was about a year old I could punch, bite and elbow and by eighteen months I'd started kicking, stamping and headbutting. This might sound a little bit hardcore to some people but it was simply a matter of survival. A quick argument would take place first – an accusation of some kind probably, or just an insult – and then, once we'd got all that preliminary crap out of the way, it would be straight down to business – BOOM! It was toddler warfare. We'd start off in the living room, punching, kicking and throwing each other off the furniture and then once we'd become tired of using our limbs to inflict injury we'd go looking for weapons. Things like remote controls were always the first to hand but the damage you could do with one of those was limited so in an act of desperation we'd try picking up chairs or even the bloody coffee table. There was a lot of shouting, a shit load of swearing and lots of cries of 'AAAAAAAAAARGH!'

Once we'd exhausted the living room a natural break would occur when we'd catch our breath and try to think of the location of some suitable – and preferably lethal – weaponry. One by one we'd go darting off to wherever the arms were concealed and then once we were all tooled up and back in the room it would start again.

'Right you bastard! Now I'm going to kill you. AAAAAAAARGH!'

I remember our dad used to have a replica samurai sword and whoever managed to get their hands on that first obviously had the upper hand. Or the upper cut, if you like. We used to chase each other around the house with this and the only thing that prevented us from taking a swipe and probably killing each other was the fact that it weighed quite a bit so we couldn't swing it properly. Eventually Dad realised what was happening and locked the thing away and it's a damn good job he did as I shudder to think what might have happened otherwise.

Our mum must have had the patience of a stadium full of saints when dealing with us. As we became older and stronger it obviously became more and more difficult to split us up and so in the end she would just put each of us in one of the bedrooms hoping that we'd play quietly. She should have done that from the off, really. Either that or just sedated us.

Unfortunately, this boisterous behaviour wasn't just confined to home and even a quick trip to the shops would often turn nasty. I know that all brothers fight a bit but that's all we ever did. There was never any downtime. Or, if there was, it was simply the calm before the next storm. Mum and Dad recently reminded me of a day trip to Blackpool we tried to make in the early 1990s. Notice I say 'tried' to make. Apparently, we had an Austin Montego at the time which means sod all to me but one of the reasons Mum and Dad had bought the car was because it had two rear-facing seats in the boot so that me, Alex and James wouldn't have to sit next to each other. Nice try! It was going to take more than a couple of rear-facing seats to stop the war. Even though we weren't able to hit each other we could still have a go verbally. And we did. Threats of what we'd do to each other once we reached Blackpool began being issued before we'd even left our road and by the time we reached junction 19 of the M6, which was about twenty-five miles from home, Dad had had enough.

'THAT'S IT! WE'RE GOING HOME.'

At first I think we thought it was just an idle threat and so we carried on. It wasn't, though. Dad was serious, and who can blame him? Sure enough, he came off at junction 19, went straight around the roundabout, and started heading back to Stoke.

'I'm not putting up with that for another eighty miles,' he said. 'No way!'

In an act of defiance, Alex, James and I bawled our fucking eyes out all the way home and made far more noise than we had done arguing. Poor Dad was at the end of his tether by the time we got back and he had to lock himself in a room for a few hours. I'm surprised he didn't stay there longer. So much for a family day out.

Despite the aggro, we have always been a very close family – very pro each other – and, although I didn't know it at the time, the fighting would pay dividends once I was let loose onto the streets. Since the pottery industry disappeared, Stoke-on-Trent has become quite a deprived area. In order to survive, you have two choices: hide away and keep yourself to yourself or become street-wise and be prepared to put the boot in when necessary. I obviously chose the latter and if I hadn't had that apprenticeship in extreme violence and savagery I'd have found it very, very hard indeed.

Something that really exemplifies my choice – not to mention my mindset, back then – is the content of my very earliest memory. I must have been about three and a half years old and still at nursery and I remember this kid came up to me and started pissing me off. I can't remember what he did exactly but I remember telling him to fuck off. Even then I was using some pretty industrial language but that was the norm, not just in our house, but in the entire city. The kid went off to get a teacher and after I'd been duly reprimanded the little bastard slyly said something else to me and so I headbutted him and gave him a black eye. Headbutting has always been a speciality of mine and even at three and a half years old I was up there with the best of them. I may not have been very tall at the time but put me on a box and I could have floored an adult. Fortunately, that's not my only memory from childhood, but it's definitely my earliest. A psychologist would probably have a field day with something like that.

I think what also helped in preparing me for life on the streets was the fact that at home there was never any hiding place. So regardless of what age you were you had no choice other than to stand there and defend yourself. It didn't matter what the other one had in his hands (bar a samurai sword!); you had to put your head down and have a go, and that's exactly what we did. Once again it was fight or flight and the latter was never, ever an option – nor would you ever want to take it. Even when Mum put us in different rooms we'd still walk around like miniature caged beasts, shouting and banging on the doors. There was no retreat, no surrender, and very little by way of defence. It was as if we'd all been stuck in attack mode.

One of the things that encouraged us to behave like that, I think, was the fact that we never established a dialogue between us. So instead of saying 'Can I play with that toy?' or 'Are you going to eat that fish finger?', we simply took the toy or ate the fish finger. The victim would obviously respond to this in kind and there you would have it – constant fucking chaos! Mum and Dad used to intervene occasionally, but even then, we'd be back scrapping within a few seconds.

Mum, who is one of the world's greatest human beings, was always the peacemaker – encouraging us to shake hands and be nice to each other – and Dad was the loud authoritarian character who would just explode when he'd had enough. He's a big lad, my old man – about six foot two inches – and once he'd reached his cut-off point you knew about it. In that respect, I'm exactly the same as him, as when I do lose my rag I go nuclear, but because I've also inherited some of Mum's patience I can generally prevent myself from getting into trouble. Well, sometimes.

The other thing, apart from aggro – and a bit of love, it has to be said – that was prevalent in the Hall household was competition, and that too has served me well over the years, although more so since I took up sport.

It was there from day one really and, again, it was all a result of good old-fashioned sibling rivalry. According to Mum, I'd watch James and Alex walking when I was baby and as soon as I was able to copy them, I was off. What eventually changed was the fact that, instead of simply wanting to emulate my brothers, I wanted to beat the bastards, and so that obviously added to the tension within the household. If they ran to the end of the garden in ten seconds, I'd want to do it in nine, and if they jumped off a wall, I'd have to find a higher one. It became a bit of an obsession with me.

What also made things interesting was our height. I'm taller than James and Alex (Alex is about five foot eleven inches, James is six foot and I'm six foot three inches) and from the age of about five until I got to high school we were all roughly the same height. This meant that nobody was at a disadvantage. It also presented us with another opportunity to piss each other off and for a time that became the big motivator. Fortunately, we started to appreciate how futile that was and so we began to concentrate on our own ambitions. The rivalry was always bubbling somewhere underneath though.

Genetically, I think we have my mother to thank for our competitiveness as – in addition to retraining to become a firefighter a few years ago after spending years teaching kids with special needs – she's also started competing in Iron Man Triathlons. For those of you who don't know, this consists of a 2.4-mile swim, a 112-mile bike ride and then a full marathon. That takes some serious training and dedication and she's more than a match for it. Part of Mum's motivation is a simple desire to keep fit but she's certainly not there just to make up the numbers and that, I think, is really what drives her on.

I've never asked her about this but if I were a betting man – and I am – I'd say that one of the reasons Mum sometimes left the three of us to get on with trying to compete with each other (and it did become a bit ridiculous at times) was because she was hoping we'd develop a desire to succeed. If that *was* her modus operandi, it worked. But what separates me from Alex and James is the fact that I've always taken this hunger to achieve to ridiculous extremes. In fact, that's a pretty accurate description for me. A ridiculous extreme.

Anyway, let's get onto Dad.

Since becoming a strongman I've had to sacrifice all kinds of things – time with my family being the most troublesome and upsetting – but this is really small fry to what my old man has given up. He worked as a health and safety officer in the same factory for over twenty-five years and because of the hours he worked we hardly ever saw him. Even when we did see Dad he was stressed out; a direct consequence of coming home from a job that was repetitive and unchallenging and going straight into a warzone.

He didn't have time for hobbies or anything and because he's got a good brain on him that must have been extremely stifling. There was no 'me time' for Dad and no shed to disappear to. Because he remained dedicated to his job we were not only able to live in a nice house and never want for anything, but we were also free to get out there and try to realise our potential, knowing that – unless it was something dangerous or stupid – we would always receive his and Mum's full support. Basically, we got everything Dad should have had but couldn't, which is why I cringe sometimes when I think about the way we used to behave. Fancy walking into that, day after day. Some lesser men wouldn't have come home, but not Dad. He was obviously a glutton for punishment – thank God.

The saving grace with regards to our relationship with Dad was our annual family holiday, and because of his endeavours we were able to go to some really special places. It was the one time during the year we'd be able to spend time with him in a relaxed atmosphere. Portugal always seemed to be our family's destination of choice back then and we'd spend all day every day just chilling by the pool, having barbecues and lazing on the beach. Even the fighting used to lessen a bit during these special times and that was solely because we were all so pleased to see Dad carefree and happy for a while. He was a completely different person on holiday and that change in mood was wonderfully contagious.

Once we were back home, things would return to normal pretty quickly and before you could say 'seconds out, round one', the three amigos would be making up for lost time by smashing remote controls over each other's head, issuing death threats and making our ever-patient mother's life an absolute misery. I expect Dad was relieved to get back to work.

As well as spending some quality time with my family, those holidays taught me a very important lesson in life and that is to be grateful for what you have and to always look for the positives, however well hidden they are. The human brain will generally err toward the negative and that can often cloud your better judgement. That's something that's helped me, not just as a human being but as an athlete. When your brain's telling you that something's crap and that your life's a pile of shit, the chances are the thought is exactly that, a pile of shit.

I think Mum and Dad knew that one day the fighting would come to an end and, bar moving us all to a sodding zoo, there was bugger all they could do about it until then. Sure enough, when we got to our early teens – or when I did – we gave up fighting almost overnight and suddenly started talking to one another. We became mates, I suppose, and it's been exactly the same ever since. We still had our moments, of course, but because we'd finally learned how to talk to one another and show an interest in each other's lives, the fighting was usually averted and conversations took place instead. Pretty sweary ones, it has to be said, but conversations just the same. I remember thinking to myself after talking to Alex one day, *Wow! My brother's not a snivelling arsehole after all. He's actually OK.*

But if that was a revelation for the three of us – and it was – what must it have been like for Mum and Dad? To be honest, I think it was just a massive relief. In fact, it probably knocked years off them. Like an early retirement! They're great though, and all three of us think the sun shines out of their fu ... We think the world of them.

CHAPTER 2
Injury Time

Believe it or not, one of my first talents as a young child was having injuries and accidents. In fact, if I ever have to write a CV it's something I'll probably include.

CURRENT JOB: PROFESSIONAL STRONGMAN

SPECIAL SKILLS: STABBING MYSELF AND FALLING ARSE OVER TIT

All kids have accidents, of course, but from the age of about four onwards I seemed to develop a knack, and although this may sound strange I think I became addicted to them. It won't surprise you to know that one of my very first injuries, which was definitely *not* an accident, was perpetrated by the only person I can honestly say that I was scared of as a small child – my brother James. He was an absolute headcase from the year dot and as well as being my hero, in a way (as was Alex), he was also my nemesis.

The injury James inflicted on me was caused by him throwing ice in my face, the bastard. It was close range too, so there was never any question of it being an accident. The only thing I do question is whether or not he sharpened the ice before he threw it because it made a real mess of my face and I had stitches everywhere.

How much of it was already within me I'm not altogether sure, but these unending battles with James either established or aroused in me an almost impenetrable sense of bravery, which, on some occasions, has enabled me to take on multitudes of men without even batting an eyelid. I can honestly say that since overcoming my fear of fighting James I have never once gone into a scrap feeling scared, regardless of the numbers or the situation. Excited? Oh yes. Exhilarated? Definitely. But that raw emotion of fear, which can often be crippling, is something that deserted me long ago and was immediately replaced by a feeling of self-assurance. I actually felt invincible from the age of about four, which is ridiculous when you think about it. This is something that has been growing within me ever since then and as well as becoming an intrinsic part of my weaponry it is probably the one thing that separates me from my competitors in strongman. That, and being absolutely fucking excellent, of course. People may only have been calling me 'The Beast' for the last couple of years, but I think I've been one for least twenty-five.

My next mishap of note involves me falling out of a tree and although you might think this quite a standard childhood injury, I can promise you it was anything but.

James was with me – naturally – and I think we'd challenged each other as to who could climb the highest. Because I was now confident *and* competitive, I just kept on going while James had the good sense to stop. Even when I knew I'd climbed higher than he had and I was running out of tree, I refused to stop. Eventually one of the branches snapped and down I came. I must have fallen at least thirty or forty feet and the faster I fell the harder I hit the branches, and the closer I got to the ground the bigger and harder the branches became. By the time I eventually landed I was in all kinds of agony, and as well as a broken arm I had bumps on my head the size of bull's testicles and was covered in about a hundred bruises.

My immediate reaction was to call to James and ask him to get Mum and Dad, but as he ran off in the direction of the house I suddenly started to laugh. I had never, ever felt pain like it before yet in a strange sort of way I almost enjoyed it. I remember saying to myself, *This is fucking brilliant!* I'd just fallen out of a massive tree and had survived. It felt like an achievement.

A minute or so later, as I started to relive what had happened, an overwhelming sense of excitement surged through my body, almost cancelling out the pain, and I swear that if I had been physically able to I would have climbed the tree and done it again.

Does that make me sound a bit weird? I suppose it does but then I probably am a bit. You have to be, if you're going to be me.

The next incident is a little bit gorier and took place on a family holiday to Portugal when I was five. As well as Mum,

Dad and the three of us brothers, we also had Dad's parents with us, Grandad and Grandma, and as far as I remember the first few days were great: it was red hot and the pool was massive. Or at least it was to me.

One afternoon, about four or five days into the holiday, Grandad decided he wanted an orange and proceeded to peel one in the kitchen, with me watching him, unobserved. I don't think I'd ever seen anybody peel an orange with a knife before and remember thinking, *Good skills, Grandad!* I was amazed by the way the skin came off in one continuous twirl and it can't have taken him more than a few seconds. Shortly after he'd finished he left the room and I decided to give it a go myself. After taking an orange from the fruit bowl I pulled up a stool from the breakfast bar, took the knife from the sink and as I tried to stick the knife into the orange, it went straight through my left hand. Within about a second the orange was blood-red and there were people absolutely everywhere. It was chaos. The knife Grandad had used was thin and razor sharp so it was never going to end happily. That said, it went through my hand very easily and so when Dad pulled it out it wasn't a problem.

As opposed to taking me to hospital, which would have meant claiming on the insurance, my grandma stitched up my hand using a very fine needle and I don't remember there being any tears at all. In fact, she coped very well! Well done, Grandma. It honestly didn't bother me though and because the gash wasn't too big the pain was minimal. Most kids would have been vomiting and screaming their little arses off but it was water off a duck's back to me. I'm not trying to make myself sound tough, by the way. I'm not into all that bollocks and I've got nothing whatsoever to prove. It was just the way I was. It's always the inconvenience of being injured that bothers me most, as opposed to the injury itself.

A few days later, whilst still in Portugal, we were about to go for a walk and as I was sat on the tiled floor putting on my sandals, my dad, who was wearing clogs at the time – although don't ask me why – stood on one of my fingers by mistake and completely ripped off my fingernail. Imagine a size 11 solid wood clog with about sixteen stone of man standing in it suddenly landing on your fingernail. That particular episode was definitely less enjoyable than the tree or the orange and I remember getting a kick up the arse for calling Dad a ... something quite rude.

From the point of view of simply staying alive, the worst thing that could have happened to me at this time was finding somebody even more dangerous to emulate than James and Alex, but that's exactly what did happen.

In truth, it was only a character from a film, but the man who played him went on to become my biggest inspiration outside of my family. As well as being lucky enough to have met the great man in later life, I was also proud to have him present at two of my deadlift records; he was actually at my side cheering me on at both of them. He is the incredible Mr Arnold Schwarzenegger and when I was about five years old his most iconic film role gave me somewhere to channel all of this confidence, energy and bravery that was running through my five-stone frame. I almost died in the process, but it felt great!

The fictional character in question is obviously the Terminator and over the years I must have watched the film at least a hundred times. I actually think it was still an eighteen certificate back then so I started watching it a good thirteen years early. Mum and Dad would have had a fit if they'd found out but I'm so glad they didn't.

Like millions of other kids, I wanted to *be* Arnolds Schwarzenegger's seemingly indestructible cybernetic android and after becoming completely and utterly obsessed with the character I set about trying to copy him and even made up some of my own stunts. These included throwing myself off bikes at high speed, jumping off high walls and trying to land on one foot, and even throwing myself out of trees instead of just falling out of them. Looking back it must have seemed like I had some kind of death wish but I remember feeling so pumped up at having something to aim towards.

Mmmmm. I think I needed to go to school!

CHAPTER 3

Educating Eddie

I think my parents were hoping that school might tame me a bit and, despite me not being the ideal pupil, it probably did for the first few months. I was obviously out of my comfort zone a bit and without my brothers being there I had to establish myself as an individual.

Educationally I was a bit of a paradox, I suppose, because as well as being easily distracted I was also the one most willing to try. Regardless of whether I knew the answer or not I would always be the first to put my hand up when the teacher asked a question. If I didn't know the answer, I'd just guess – but I had to be the first. I obviously wasn't a shy boy but my main motivation wasn't getting the question right, it was seeking the approval of others. So whenever I did manage to answer a question correctly and was congratulated by the teacher I'd almost explode with pride. That's something that has never left me. Even today, if I win a competition, a text from my mum saying 'Well done son, I'm proud of you' will mean more to me than any trophy. Making people proud or pleased, however trivial the situation or the circumstances, is the main reason I do what I do.

With regards to my behaviour at primary school, let's just say that it was a game of two halves. My first school, Friarswood, is undoubtedly a wonderful educational establishment now but twenty-odd years ago my group of mates would be there telling the teachers to fuck off. Every break time there'd be a big group of us – seven, eight and nine year olds – smoking behind the bike sheds and fighting each other ... these were the kids I always gravitated towards and them to me.

It wasn't that I necessarily liked many of them. They were just a lot more exciting than the bright kids and the one thing I couldn't live without was excitement. When I was with my brothers there was never, ever a dull moment and when they both went to school I was bored shitless. Being with kids full-time again made me want to try to replicate what my brothers and I had at home. Although it was never the same as it was with Alex and James, it was better than sitting on my own or with a load of uncool boffins.

The only real bright spot throughout my entire sentence at Friarswood was my reception teacher, Mrs Vivian Mills. She was like a beacon of positivity and calmness in a period of my life that I considered to be a massive inconvenience, but because she only taught me during my first year at the school her influence sadly wore off pretty quickly. When Mrs Mills spoke, everybody sat up and listened. Not because she was commanding (although she was), but because she always had something interesting to say. That much I do remember. Unbeknownst to me, Mrs Mills must have followed my progress in strongman and when I finally went professional back in 2014 she tracked me down and handed me a cheque for £200.

'I read that you'd gone professional Eddie,' she said giving me a peck on the cheek. 'So here's something to help you on your way.'

It was fabulous seeing her again and was an amazing gesture. That's the mark of the woman and people like her change lives. Luckily for me, she wasn't the only person who was to have a positive influence on me during these years.

One of my parents' many attempts at giving me an interest other than roughhousing and inflicting injury was offering me piano lessons when I was nine. I don't mind admitting that I was horrified when they first suggested it. I was a miniature thug for Christ's sake, whose hobbies included smashing bottles over people's heads and using four-letter words beginning with F and C. I couldn't think of anything more diametrically opposed to what I enjoyed doing than learning a flaming instrument, which was probably the reason Mum and Dad tried to get me into it. Piano lessons! I could have died.

My teacher, who lived on our street, was called Mrs Winder and she and her husband had lived in the area for years. She must have been in her sixties at the time and when I turned up for my first lesson I was, not to put too fine a point on it, somewhat lacking in enthusiasm.

'You must be Eddie,' she said on opening the door. 'Come on in.'

Mrs Winder had a very kind face and from the moment I set eyes on her I felt completely at ease. This wasn't how I was used to feeling when I met new people. Something was obviously wrong.

'Before we start, let's have a quick chat,' said Mrs Winder. 'I want to know all about you.'

Again, that wasn't how people spoke to me.

'All right then,' I said. 'What do you want to know?'

After asking me some questions about school and stuff, Mrs Winder turned the conversation to music.

'Do you like music, Eddie?' she said.

I just shrugged. 'Only the Beatles,' I answered truthfully. 'Mum and Dad used to play them in the car.'

'OK then. Let's see if we can find something you like.'

By this time I remember thinking that I didn't want to play the piano or listen to music, I just wanted to carry on talking to Mrs Winder. I've always enjoyed the company of older people and there was something about her I really liked.

'Tell me what you think of this,' she said, before picking out some music and sitting down at the piano.

The tune she played was 'Love Me Do' by the Beatles and I grinned from ear to ear as I began to recognise what she was playing.

'It's the Beatles,' I said approvingly.

'That's right,' said Mrs Winder. 'If you practise hard enough you might be able to play that one day.'

That was all the incentive I needed and over the next two years or so I became quite a proficient little pianist. Impatient, but then isn't every child when they start learning a new instrument? In the end I could turn my hand to most styles of music but I always ended up playing either the Beatles or John Lennon. 'Imagine' was my favourite. It still is.

What was even more enjoyable than the music – and, in all honesty, was the reason I stuck it out for so long – was my unique friendship with Mrs Winder. It might sound slightly ridiculous to some people but going to her house became one of the highlights of my week and, as much as I enjoyed tickling the ivories and paying homage to the Fab Four, it was the conversation running alongside that fired me and caught my imagination. Mrs Winder and I would talk throughout each lesson and I'd tell her things that I wouldn't dream of telling my parents, or even my friends for that matter. No subject ever seemed to be off limits and I knew that whatever truths or revelations I divulged would never go any further. Mrs Winder knew that I was a bit of a tearaway but there was obviously something about me she liked and knowing that made me feel great.

The lessons were like a cross between a confessional and a counselling session and in hindsight I should have carried them on into adulthood. In fact, if you're still alive, Mrs Winder, get in touch!

Chapter 3

Domestically, there was only one person who could bring out the best in me without trying, and that was Nan my mum's mum. As much as I love my parents, they obviously represented authority and because they had to spend so much of their time telling me off and answering letters from school, our relationship was often fraught.

Being with Nan, though, was like being wrapped in a warm blanket. Whenever I was with her all the anger I felt just disappeared. In every other situation there'd be aggro of some kind bubbling underneath but with her it was different. I could never scowl at my nan like I'd scowl at Mum and Dad. It was just unthinkable. I only smiled when I was with her.

Occasionally she'd offer me little bits of advice and if she'd heard about me being naughty she'd smile at me and say, 'Eeee, what have you been up to now, Eddie?' She never judged me. In fact, I don't remember Nan ever judging anybody.

What she gave me more than anything was unconditional love and for somebody who pissed a lot of people off and had a lot of things going on in his head that was incredibly important. It didn't matter how many people I'd infuriated or how aggrieved I felt, Nan's love would wash it all away. She was my lifeblood.

By the time I got to Year Five at Friarswood I'd burned my bridges so badly that I had to be moved to a different school. My confidence, or should I say cockiness, had been overflowing again since I'd found my feet there and together with limitless amounts of courage, a mouth like an open sewer and an overwhelming compulsion to piss people off I had officially become public enemy number one. If my parents hadn't moved me when they did I'd either have been expelled by the headmaster, bumped off by a contract killer hired by the PTA, or set upon by a group of desperate, rabid teachers.

The straw that broke the camel's back was probably fighting. It had always been a problem for me at Friarswood but by the time I'd been there a few years it had become an epidemic and each and every playtime I'd be involved in some kind of gang warfare somewhere in the school. Unfortunately this would often follow me back into the classroom and that's when the trouble really started. You see, the kids I fought at school were the same kids I fought outside of school and so there was a constant undercurrent of hostility there that would occasionally morph into violence. We're not talking about simple fisticuffs here. Even at six or seven we were using bottles and large pieces of wood. Anything we could get out hands on, basically, and I used to love every single second of it. I genuinely was the proverbial little bastard, I'm afraid, but as a firm believer in karma it was all part and parcel of becoming who I am today. That's my excuse, anyway.

The next school daft enough to have me was Westlands Primary School in Newcastle-under-Lyme but my experiences there were very different to Friarswood with regards to the teachers, the pupils and everyone's general behaviour and the contrast took me by surprise.

My own teacher especially, Mr Stirland, was on a completely different level to any adult I'd ever met before and the effect he had on me was both immediate and profound. Together with my reception teacher Mrs Mills, my nan, and one or two others, he was one of a select few adults who was able to influence me as a child and prevent me from acting like a prick. He was one of those teachers that you never, ever forget and he was actually the first, after my nan, to discipline me using words that weren't either shouted or screamed. He simply spoke in a soft but commanding voice.

At first I didn't know what the bloody hell to do. I think I'd probably told him to fuck off or something, but instead of receiving the usual tirade in return he just sat me down and talked to me. Funnily enough, it was actually *what* he said that made a difference, not how he said it. He explained in a consultative yet authoritative manner why it wasn't appropriate for me to behave in that way, and by the time he'd finished, I felt about two inches high. It was a revelation in a way and, although it didn't stop me from swearing at adults ever again, he made me pick and choose my moments. Mr Stirland also never seemed to get angry, which took the wind out of my sails, and he had a command of the English language that most of us could never dream of having. Instead of writing books, he used his gift to control – and then educate – little arseholes like me.

Although they'd often tried, nobody had ever really got the better of me before, either physically or verbally, so not only did I respect Mr Stirland massively for having achieved that, I always did as he asked. He didn't just introduce me to a different kind of behaviour, he introduced me to a different kind of *being*. He showed me there were bright people who used their brains instead of their fists in life.

From an educational point of view, Mr Stirland was again a revelation. As well as making me appreciate the importance of studying, he made it both interesting and fun. At Friarswood I'd always been seen as a potentially smart kid who just wouldn't apply himself, but because of the way Mr Stirland controlled me – and he did actually control the way I behaved – I very quickly started realising some of this potential. I could still be a little bit unruly at times and was often extremely cheeky, but that was par for the course. Mr Stirland was a teacher with gentle touch and an impressive vocabulary, not a fucking miracle worker.

One thing that also made a big difference to me was the fact that I had to call Mr Stirland 'sir'. That was the norm at Westlands and it set a precedent with me, one that I enjoyed being a part of. A lot of people won't believe this but I actually have a tremendous amount of respect for discipline, providing it's explained to me concisely and I consider it to be fair. Present me with the opposite, however, and I'll kick up a massive fuss. Not because I'm difficult, but because I refuse to take shit from people.

Over the next year or so, Westlands Primary School became a kind of educational enclave for me and after just a few weeks of being there I repaid Mr Stirland's faith and hard work by getting myself in the top sets for everything. I went from being a little shit to a scholar and it was a very satisfying transformation.

Whilst me infiltrating the top sets at school was a miracle to some people, to others it was an abomination. Some of the brighter pupils thought I was a bit of a dickhead (although they didn't say as much) and once I started invading their territory they were horrified.

'How the hell did someone like you make it into Set One?' one of them asked me. 'You're always misbehaving.'

My reply was typically to the point.

'Because I'm fucking clever.'

It was true, I was, but the best was yet to come. About half way through Year Six the top seven or eight pupils from my year were invited to take the exam to attend one of the local private schools and I was one of them. This, I think, was the final insult to those boffins who disapproved of me and when word got around I could see that they were absolutely disgusted. Things like this weren't meant to happen to people like me, and that, brothers and sisters, could actually end up being my epitaph! Proving people wrong has actually become a bit of an addiction to me and even back then it felt absolutely fantastic. But what felt even better than getting one over on those dickheads was finding my feet as a human being – or starting to – and realising that there were other avenues worth exploring apart from just messing about.

I think most kids have got it in them to do well at school, providing they're in the right environment and surrounded by the right people. Unfortunately, not all of them are lucky enough to have those essentials but I'm living proof that they can make a real difference to a child. If I'd stayed at Friarswood, God knows where I'd have ended up. Behind bars, probably. There was still time for me to mess things up, though, as I'd prove at high school. My problem was that in order to stay on the straight and narrow I needed Mr Stirland to be there twenty-four hours a day and that was obviously never going to happen.

One thing that did help to reinforce Mr Stirland's influence on me was joining the Cubs. I'd already been a Beaver from the age of six until eight but I remember Cubs being much more fun and once I started going to Westlands it almost became an extension of school. A lot of my new classmates went to Cubs and so that too gave me an incentive to calm down a bit and behave. One thing I noticed at Cubs, more than I did school, was that because I was big and because I liked a fight, a lot of kids tended to gravitate towards me. Even at the age of eight I was very much the alpha male. I definitely thrived on that kind of attention and adulation and it was something that I was very keen to build on and preserve. Part of that was down to simply wanting to be the top dog, and the other part was wanting people's approval. Whenever we went camping I always wanted to be the one who put up the tent and built the fire and the reward for me pushing myself forward and doing that was the aforementioned approval. That made me a very happy boy.

CHAPTER 4

Swimming Against the Stream

Unfortunately, school and Cubs only took up about half of my waking hours, which meant there was still plenty of time for me to get myself into trouble. In this respect I never, ever wasted a minute and as the battles got harder, so did I. Despite my persona in the classroom and in the church hall, my natural setting was and always had been 'head case', and unfortunately no amount of outdoor activity or academia could overshadow that. 'A loose cannon' was how one teacher once referred to me and even though I couldn't stand the old bugger he'd hit the nail on the head.

Fortunately, there was still one final saving grace that took up just enough of that spare time to keep me out of the correction centres. It's something I became obsessed with for a while and am still good at to this day, although given the size of me you might not think so. That something is swimming and for a while I was one of the country's brightest young hopes. As well as setting records here, there and everywhere, and winning loads of gold medals, I was tipped as being a future Olympian. Sadly, my slightly wayward personality and inability to conform – or in other words, my big gob – prevented me from taking it as far as it could have gone and I think it's something my parents still regret.

According to Mum, I first started swimming way back in 1990 on one of our treasured holidays to Portugal. Back then, during the last two weeks in June, there was something called the Potters' Fortnight, which was Stoke's version of the Wakes Week holiday, and Grandad and Grandma had treated us all to a fortnight away. This would have been our very first holiday as a family and even though I was just two years old I was already trying to emulate my brothers in the pool. They were both good swimmers and in order to match them I would first have to become armband-free. To me this wasn't a problem but to Mum it was, and every time I jumped into the swimming pool and ripped them off she would scoop me out and put them back on again. This battle of aquatic attrition went on for absolutely ages – it happened about twenty times, apparently – until eventually Mum just said, 'Right then, you. I've had enough of this. Sink or swim.' And apparently, I swam. Well, I say I swam. It was probably more of a doggie paddle really, but it was a start.

Mum's actually a qualified swimming instructor and although she's taught one or two kids who've been able to swim at two, it definitely wasn't the norm. I don't think it was natural ability that enabled me to stay afloat, although that did come into effect later on. Instead the main impetus definitely came from a desire to catch up with my brothers. But what's more significant to the present day, and in particular to becoming a strongman, is that I managed to do it all on my own. Working things out for myself and being a self-starter have been the foundations on which I have been able to build my career as a strongman and that self-contained attitude was as important to me as a kid as it is today.

Swimming, as well as being my hobby, was the only sport I was ever interested in as a child. In fact, it was my life. Even when I was just five years old I remember seeing all the other kids running home after school and while they were all sitting around playing on their PlayStation eating cornflakes I'd be down the pool for an hour and a half swimming my arse off. Up and down I went, night after night after night. It didn't matter what the weather was like or what was on TV, swimming was all I thought about. I still turned into a savage again the moment I left the pool but for as long as I was in the water the people of Newcastle could walk about in relative safely.

Although I was part of a club from the age of five, I started competitive swimming from the age of about eight. Once again I took it all very, very seriously and always made sure that I learned from my experiences. I remember missing lunch once for some reason one day and although the difference wasn't massive I was definitely below par at training, so from then on I made sure that I never missed a meal. Following on from that I started watching what I ate, so even at eight and nine I was eating and training like an athlete. Or at least like I thought an athlete should. I remember reading interviews with Mark Foster and the more I read the more obsessed I became and the more obsessed I became the more I started altering my behaviour. I didn't tell my parents or my swimmimg teacher about this. I just got on with it. The first thing I did each morning after getting out of bed was a ten-minute stretch, which Mark Foster had said was important for mobility. Well, if it was good enough for Mark, it was good enough for me. I'm not sure why I didn't want anybody else to know but I remember teaching myself to stretch very, very quietly. It isn't possible for me to do anything by halves and because of my obsessive nature and relentless determination to improve that always put me ahead of the game.

Once again, one of the main motivations in me becoming the next Mark Foster was that desire to beat my brothers; they were both really good competitive swimmers so I threw myself into yet another self-induced war of sibling attrition. By this point I don't think James and Alex could have given a toss about our sibling rivalry but I'm afraid I wasn't letting go quite so easily. Looking back, my obsession was probably bordering on being unhealthy. I certainly don't regret it because it's helped me get where I am, but I've never met anybody as obsessed with coming first as me. Even then I never, ever needed motivating. Everything came from within.

I think the advantage of having two older brothers for heroes is that the ultimate goal of becoming as good as them was always attainable. You don't get that with the David Beckhams of this world. That kind of hero is almost untouchable really, and getting to where they are is always difficult to envisage. My two idols were usually in their bedrooms, farting and carrying on.

I remember going to training sessions with my brothers and some other lads and if I didn't win every single length I'd go off on one. Sometimes I'd cry and sometimes I'd shake with anger. I was even physically sick once; that was how much it meant to me. It would just make me try harder and as soon as I got home I'd run upstairs to my bedroom and work out what I had to do to improve. For a young lad I was ridiculously focused, if a little bit unstable!

I started winning races at the club almost from day one and the euphoria I felt when people congratulated me was like nothing I'd ever experienced before. All somebody had to say was 'Well done, Eddie' and I'd be floating on air. Whoever said it would get a mile-wide smile and that alone would give me enough impetus to want to win again. I mean *really* want to win. Nothing I have ever drunk, eaten or smoked before has ever had such a dramatically pleasing effect and I can't see that ever changing. There's something very life-affirming about making people happy.

Chapter 4

Competitive swimming played a big role in making me who I am today, and I can honestly say I loved it. Unfortunately, though, I also had the little matter of school to attend to. My primary school years were coming to an end and now high school was rearing its ugly head on the horizon. But first, a little holiday ...

CHAPTER 5

The School of Hard Knocks

A few months before I started at high school we went on a two-week family holiday to Kenya. Yes, you heard right. Although we lived on a nice street we were probably the ones with the least amount of money, and while everyone was driving around in Mercs and the like we still had our clapped-out Austin Montego. What a shitheap that was! But it was all a case of priorities: instead of Mum and Dad spending their hard-earned cash on a new car, which my brothers and I would only have ended up wrecking, they decided to take us away to nice places and make some memories.

Kenya, though. That was a very different ball game and I was ridiculously excited when they told us. The reason I'm mentioning it is because – as well as it being the best holiday we ever had as a family – it also taught me a life lesson that, if I'm totally honest, gave me a much-needed kick up the arse.

What happened was this. While we were out in Africa we were invited by our rep, who was Kenyan, to play football at one of the local schools and afterwards somebody handed me a packet of sweets. Within about two seconds I had a hundred hands in my face and a few seconds after that, no sweets. At the time I was a bit angry and complained to the person who'd handed them to me.

'Hey,' I said to him. 'I didn't have one of those sweets.'

Straightaway he looked at me as if I was stupid. 'They weren't for you,' he said. 'They were for them.'

Like most kids who are brought up in places like the UK, I was full of my own self-importance but that changed the way I thought and made me pull my head out of my arse. Apparently the world didn't revolve around me after all. It was a small incident but it made a big impression on me.

This wasn't the only experience that created a lasting memory for me on that holiday. While we were there we went on safari and saw elephants, lions and giraffes in the wild, but the highlight for me actually happened at a zoo. We were in the reptile house and one of the keepers told me to cup my hands and hold them out. Then he handed me an egg.

'Be very, very careful with it,' he said. 'If you keep it warm, it might hatch.'

'What's inside it?' I asked him.

'It's a crocodile,' he said.

Just then the bloody egg began to hatch and within about thirty seconds I had a newborn crocodile lying in the palm of my hand! Things like that don't happen in Stoke. Although I did have a dead rat thrown at me once.

Anyway, I can't avoid high school any longer so we may as well crack on with it.

Somebody asked me the other day if, after leaving primary school, I felt ready to go to high school, and I replied, 'Is anybody ever ready?' Going from being top dog to the lowest of the low is hard to take and in my case the thought of starting all over again *and* being in education for another five years filled me with dread. The inspirational Mr Stirland had a new batch of idiots to teach and my new place of learning made Friarswood Primary look like a Swiss finishing school. The importance of learning hadn't left me yet but I hated my new high school. I thought it was dog rough.

When I started at high school, James was in Year Nine and if he hadn't been there I would have been in a lot of trouble. Kids in the older years were always picking fights with the biggest guys in the years below and I would have been just what they were looking for. James, who had a fierce reputation but did very well in class, prevented that from happening, which meant I could crack on and make some new friends. These, not surprisingly, were all the kids who used to get caught smoking and that became the status quo for the entire time I was there. Although I wasn't much of a smoker myself, I did enjoy the odd spliff and for the first couple of years at high school – that is, when I was around eleven and twelve

– I did little else. Even after school, the first thing we'd do was go straight to the park to get wasted, which was daft really because that wasn't me at all. I did it partly because it was something I wanted to experience but the main reason was because I was desperate to fit in. These were the people I'd chosen to hang out with and, as mad as it might sound, I gave them exactly the same commitment I'd given to training. I got stuck in! I was also the alpha male, remember, and was naturally compelled to lead from the front. There were one or two kids who were slightly taller than me in class but because of my endeavours in the swimming pool I was built like the proverbial brick shithouse and had already been the proud owner of a six-pack for about four years. I must have been at least five foot eleven inches when I started at high school so aesthetically I had the same physical attributes as an adult; I was just broader-shouldered and generally thinner.

A few years previously, while I was at Friarswood Primary, some of the pupils accused me of taking performance enhancing drugs because I was so ripped. The name-calling went on for weeks on end but to me it was simply a tribute to what I'd achieved. Every time one of them shouted something I just smiled my well-developed little arse off. They thought I needed to take drugs to look like I did and that made me feel unique. I remember thinking, *Fucking right, mate, I am something special!*

It's often been said, usually in a negative way, that people who are driven can be quite narcissistic. But I think it's a requirement rather than a trait and it doesn't necessarily mean you're a prick. Do I have an excessive interest in myself and my physical appearance, which, according to the dictionary, are the attributes that signify a narcissist? Well, of course I do, and have done from a very early age. My body and my personality are my livelihood, though, so it's no different from a greengrocer harping on about how great his shop is.

The best two examples I can think of with regards to people who have made this characteristic work for them are Muhammad Ali and the aforementioned Arnold Schwarzenegger.

I remember watching Arnold Schwarzenegger's film *Pumping Iron* many moons ago. It's a docudrama that follow's Arnie's journey to the 1975 Mr Olympia competition, which was being held in South Africa. I first saw it at the age of eleven and it made a huge impression on me. In the film, Arnie openly uses psychological warfare to intimidate his opponents and get under their skin. He had decided to go public as a narcissist and so instead of just being quietly confident like the other contenders he started broadcasting it to anyone who'd listen. I was completely flabbergasted by the way he spoke to people. Another one who plays similar kinds of mind games is José Mourinho. Providing you're as good as you say you are – and he, Ali and Arnold most certainly are – you have a good chance of making it work for you. OK, so you might make one or two enemies, but in actual fact the only real enemies you make are the people who you defeat, so in my opinion it's a job well done.

So by the age of eleven I was already an arrogant little bastard with an allegation of taking performance enhancing drug abuse to my name. Watching Arnold Schwarzenegger made me fall in love with being in love with myself, if that makes sense, and it's now a big part of who I am.

This insight is all fairly retrospective, by the way, as I only found out what a narcissist was a couple of years ago. Somebody called me one on social media one day and when I looked it up in the dictionary I was cock-a-fucking-hoop. I didn't reply to the prat who posted it but I remember thinking, *On the fucking nail, dickhead.* The fact that he'd called me a narcissist meant that I'd got to him in some way and that just made me happy.

It's the narcissists with no self-awareness who are the ones who annoy people and gyms are absolutely full of them. The lads with a fake tan and the Gucci vest and trainers who only train their chest and biceps. We all know a few of them and the chances are there might be one or two reading this book. Well, if you are one of those hitherto oblivious narcissists, stop being a twat and start making it work for you. And give over with the fake tan. You look like an idiot!!

Anyway, back to high school (if we must). Even though I didn't like the place and was in with the wrong crowd I still managed to utilise some of my academic potential and without trying I again managed to force myself into the top set for every single subject. I was also the class clown and so even in class all I did was dick around. Once again this vexed the arse off the poor devils who had to strive to achieve academic excellence and when their frustrations came to the fore I used to enjoy perfecting my cockiness on them. They used to get so worked up, bless them.

'Oi, Eddie. You misbehave, dick around and call everyone a twat, yet you're in all the top sets. How the hell do you do it?'

'Natural talent, mate. Some of us have it, and some of us don't. Actually, quite a few of you don't.'

This was my apprenticeship for becoming the man I am today. Fortunately, it's something you can never perfect which means you can always enjoy trying.

I felt really let down by some of my teachers at my high school. Not all of but enough were able to rid me of any remnants of enthusiasm or aptitude I may have had. In some of my more benevolent moments I have tried to persuade myself that they might have had their enthusiasm knocked out of them by teaching unruly kids for years but some of them seemed to enjoy putting pupils down. Actually, there were two in particular who, if I saw them in the street today, I'd have to stop myself from punching them in the back of the head. They seemed to go out of their way to make my life a misery and for a time they were very successful. They were always putting me down and it was as if they wanted me to fail. They know who they are and if either of them are reading this, thanks for the contribution and I hope you paid full price!

Bright or not, I still had plenty of wobbles in my early years at high school but was kept on the straight and narrow, or my unique version of the straight and narrow, by an exasperated supply teacher who I could tell wanted to kill me. He was quite calm normally, which was a novelty, and had short dark hair and a beard. Hands up, I admit I behaved like an absolute dick for this man but for the first few lessons he said nothing and just glared at me. I didn't do anything especially bad, by the way, it was just the usual clowning around. There is such a thing as having too much of a good thing though and at the end of what must have been the fourth or fifth lesson with him he asked me to stay behind. I was obviously quite used to this and as he was only a supply teacher and not one of our regulars I was expecting a quick reprimand. How wrong can you be!

When the last pupil bar me had left the classroom he got up, shut the door, walked over to where I was sitting and proceeded to tear me a brand-new arsehole. The language he used was even worse than mine and as he prodded me in the chest I could tell by the look in his eyes that all he wanted to do was take me by the scruff of the neck and shake me until my head fell off. Fortunately for me he just carried on prodding but what really held my interest was the fact that the words coming out of his mouth belied his physical slightness. He didn't seem remotely intimidated. 'What the fuck are you doing?' he said. 'Seriously, Eddie, what the fuck are you doing? Why are you making my life a misery and why are you acting like a dick? You do realise by acting like this you're fucking up everyone else's chances, don't you?'

At first I was really taken aback. I'd had teachers swear at me before but never so vociferously. I had it in my head at the time that I wanted to be a swimmer when I left school and so I didn't bother applying myself to my schoolwork at all. I was convinced I'd be going to the Olympics or whatever so I didn't really give a shit. This was my answer when he asked me if I realised what I was doing.

'You honestly think you're going to make a living from being a swimmer, Eddie,' he said. 'OK, so what if it doesn't work out? What if you get injured? What are you going to do then?'

I just shrugged when he said that, but it was definitely hitting home.

'You cannot rely on something as tenuous as swimming, Eddie, and do you know why I'm telling you this? Because you're obviously a really bright kid and if you stopped being a prat for just one second and decided to knuckle down a bit you could have a go at being a swimmer with a plan B in place. You've only got one chance, Eddie. Don't fuck it up.'

Since becoming a strongman I've been on the end of some astonishing inspirational talks, usually from my mate and fellow strongman, Rob Frampton, and this had exactly the same effect. A lot of other kids would have reported him for swearing and being a bit physical but this bloke was going out of his way to make a positive difference to my future and my God, his words hit home.

I don't even know this bloke's name, more's the pity, but I came out of that classroom a changed kid. OK, I didn't become a prefect overnight or anything, but I did knuckle down a bit for a while and tried to stop buggering up everyone else's chances. I must admit it was hard as I enjoyed making people laugh but from that day I had learned what was more important.

The subject I enjoyed and excelled at most was maths and it's something that has paid dividends as a strongman. A lot of the other kids used to hate it and could never understand its relevance but to me it seemed obvious. If somebody said, 'Why do we have to learn about angles on a triangle?' I'd reply, 'Because if you're an architect you need to be able to work out how high a roof needs to be.' That's obviously quite a crude example, but you get my drift. Maths made sense to me and it's added real value to my life as a strongman.

Today I use it for things like degrees and leverage, but in addition to that it helps me with calorie counting and working out the lengths of bars. The one that impresses people most is being able to convert pounds to kilograms, or vice versa. I don't need a calculator. It's just pops up in my head and I can do it in a flash.

568 lb = 257 kilos

See!

So if there are any aspiring strongmen or strongwomen reading this, for heaven's sake, make sure you knuckle down and get your GCSEs. You won't regret it.

CHAPTER 6

A (Swimming) Star in the Making

By the time I was twelve years old (and twelve stone) I was actually in quite a good place for a change. I was doing well at school, I'd cut down on my cannabis intake and was even having fewer fights. This would have been the same time that peace broke out between me and my brothers and to top it all off, my swimming career was coming along very nicely.

That supply teacher's lecture had had a very strange snowball effect on my mindset because the confidence I'd gained from working hard at school, and creating a safety net for if the swimming went tits up, actually gave me even more confidence in the pool. This allowed me to relax more and helped me to perform better. It was a proper paradox all right, but one that I gratefully accepted.

The only people who were suffering on my behalf now were my parents – but just for a change it was down to something I was doing right, as opposed to any misdemeanours. I was now completely dedicated to swimming, which meant they were having to take me training at all hours, and because they had such punishing jobs I could tell that it was killing them. Neither of them ever complained but I remember glancing over at them sometimes as we drove towards the swimming pool and they looked exhausted. The most punishing of these sessions started at 5.30 a.m., which meant we had to be up and out by 5 a.m. I wasn't especially happy about this either but it was purgatory to Mum and Dad.

The dedication required by young competitive swimmers is obviously significant but the same could also be said for the parents. Fancy giving up almost every bloody weekend just so your kid can go swimming. You can't really get pissed the night before a competition because the chances are you'll have to drive to God knows where at silly o'clock in the morning and then once you're there you'll be sat on your arse twiddling your thumbs for hours on end. It's a seriously hard life and because the sport's so popular and competitive, only a tiny, tiny fraction of young hopefuls make it to the Nationals, which is short for the National Age Group Championships. At the time that was my own personal ambition and even though I stood a good chance of qualifying there was no way it was going to be at the expense of my parents' sanity. I'd caused them enough grief over the years and it was about time I started paying back some of their love and dedication.

I think I'd just finished watching *The Terminator* again for what must have been about the fifteenth time and, feeling pumped-up and inspired as I always did by the end, I found

Mum and Dad and told them I had an announcement to make. God only knows what they thought I was going to say. I'd already nearly given Mum a heart attack by borrowing Dad's hair clippers and giving myself a Mohican (school were not happy!) and I think she thought I'd had something pierced or, worse, had a tattoo done. Me, have a tattoo or get something pierced? What a ridiculous suggestion.

Once I'd got Mum and Dad together I informed them of my plans.

'From now on I'm going to make my own way to training in the morning and I'll do the same for the evening session. Oh yes. And I'm going to win every single freestyle event at the 2001 Nationals.'

As statements go this was bold to say the least but Mum and Dad hardly batted an eyelid. They knew exactly how good I was and, in my own self-assured little mind, attaining the required qualifying times would be a mere formality.

Sure enough, I managed to qualify for every single race – the 50m, 100m, 200m, 400m and the 1500m – and my God, did I train for it. The regime was three and a half hours a day, five days a week, with competitions at weekends. As fit and driven as I undoubtedly was, it was damn hard work.

After getting up at 5 a.m. I'd cycle into Newcastle town centre, which was about two miles, and do a full-on ninety-minute session. Then, in the evening, I'd make the same journey again and do another two hours. My coach was a man called Arnold Faulkner who was the Head Coach at

Newcastle Swimming Club. He must have been in his fifties when I first got to know him and he had short grey hair and wore glasses. The best way of describing Arnold back then in terms of personality was firm but fair and he was the person who taught me the importance of consistency. He didn't get through to everyone though and I remember there were two other swimmers in the group who, for whatever reason, only used to turn up to the morning sessions once or maybe twice a week. While this understandably exasperated Arnold it used to infuriate me, as even though I cycled in I never missed a session. So to try and teach them a lesson, and to make them feel inadequate, I began playing games with them. Whenever they did turn up for the morning session I'd allow them to beat me, which obviously lulled them into a false sense of superiority. Then, come the weekend and the competitions, I'd completely annihilate them. They were obviously a bit miffed by this but as opposed to doing something about it they just stood there looking like dickheads week after week and carried on turning up when they wanted.

I think Arnold was secretly pleased that these lads didn't always turn up because if ever I needed an illustration of the rewards that consistency brings, that was it. Being a budding alpha male also meant that I was forever looking for opportunities to prove myself over the next man, and in that respect, it was manna from heaven. But by far the best part of training for the Nationals, or just training in general really, was feeling myself improve. What a fucking thrill that was, and still is! Back then I obviously had fewer distractions so the feelings of euphoria it gave me were very, very pure and in the run-up to the 2001 Nationals they were my lifeblood. These days it's slightly different because there are so many different factors to consider, such is the pressure of being a professional sportsman, but it still gives me a massive high. If I hadn't been so driven and confident it wouldn't have felt nearly as good because it wouldn't have meant as much, so discovering what was at the end of the rainbow was a very, very nice surprise. The ultimate reward, I suppose.

Arnold was actually the one who put the idea in my head about making my own way to training. The reason he suggested it was because one morning neither Mum or Dad had been able to take me in for some reason and, instead of getting on my bike or catching a bus, I skipped the session. The next time I saw him, Arnold said to me, 'You could make that problem go away if you cycled in. What do you think, Eddie?' This immediately got me thinking about what it was doing to Mum and Dad and a week or so later I made my announcement.

As well as being a very shrewd motivator, Arnold inspired absolute trust in me. If he said swim 100 metres in fifty-five seconds, I would swim 100 metres in fifty-five seconds, and then, if he said swim it in a minute, I'd swim it in a minute. In different circumstances, I might have questioned somebody for asking me to post a slower time, but because it was Arnold I never did. At the end of every training session he'd get us all together for a chat and whatever instructions he gave us became gospel to me. If he said we weren't drinking enough fluids, I'd start drinking more immediately and then turn up to the next session with a two-litre bottle of water in my hand; partly because I wanted to impress him, if I'm being honest, but mainly because I trusted him and relied on him to help me improve.

This might sound slightly conceited to some but because I was Arnold's star pupil, certainly with regards to commitment, but also ability and potential (OK, that does sound conceited!), I'm pretty sure he started building the training sessions around me, for the simple reason he thought I stood the best chance of success. I don't know if any of the other kids noticed it but I did. He knew he was backing a winner.

CHAPTER 7

Game Plan Emerges in Pool

Remember in one of the previous chapters I explained how I was inspired by Schwarzenegger's narcissistic persona in *Pumping Iron*, and how I started to try my own hand at projecting self-belief and unsettling my opponents? These mind games – i.e. behaviour that winds up the competition and gives me a mental edge – actually originated at swimming competitions and unfortunately they got me into all kinds of bloody trouble.

Visually, I already stuck out like a sore thumb because of my Mohican and as well as being an above-average swimmer I was also the best-looking. Easily the best-looking! Even so, this still wasn't enough for me so, as I'd done with the lads who used to skip the morning sessions, I started having some fun with my competitors. The main difference was that instead of just pissing off a couple of dickheads for a laugh like I had before, I did it because A) I wanted to fuck with my opponents' heads and gain an advantage, just like

Arnold and Ali, and B) because I was a show-off who not only enjoyed being the centre of attention but loved making people laugh. Actually, there's a C too. As you know, I also had a problem with conforming, so if an opportunity ever arose to stick two fingers up at the establishment I would grab it by the neck and shake it until I'd pissed off as many people as I could. I was the scourge of competitive swimming for a while. Seriously!

When it came to unsettling my opponents, I took my cue from Arnie. I always employed a three-pronged attack that would take place before, during and after a race and because I always won, the kids having to race me gradually became demoralised. With their performances becoming poorer, I soon became invincible.

As we lined up before a race I'd start shouting things like, 'This is going to be fucking easy,' which none of them used to like. Then, just for a bit of fun, I'd start shadow boxing and making Tarzan calls. This was the clincher really because all of a sudden, their attention was on me instead of the forthcoming race, which meant that mentally I already had them in the palm of my hand. Once the race had started, I'd always keep a metre or so behind the leaders, which made them all extremely nervous. And then, right at the last minute, I'd speed up and finish them off. The moment these also-rans were out of the pool I'd be on them, saying things like, 'I told you. Absolutely no chance, mate!' The poor fuckers didn't know what had hit them.

I'm obviously not as blasé as that these days but I still like to put my gob to good use and am more than happy to give someone the finger halfway through an event if I fancy it; partly to remind them I'm there, of course, but also to let them know that they're about to lose. People just don't know how to react to that kind of behaviour and long may that continue. Some individuals hate me for it, but they're just the people who let it get to them most. They're my prey, I suppose.

Despite the gamesmanships being a little bit unorthodox it was all within the rules and so there was bugger all anybody could do about it. I was wanted in several counties by various different kids, parents and officials, but that meant it was having the desired effect and so I just carried on. Not one of them had ever experienced anybody like me before. The thing that stopped anybody from complaining, I think, was that they all knew I was the best. If anyone had decided to kick up a fuss it would have seemed like jealousy or sour grapes. It was bordering on genius when you think about it because I was just a kid. Arnold Schwarzenegger may have been my inspiration but I still had to put meat on the bones, so to speak, and it all happened very naturally.

When it came to acting the fool, that was even more contentious, but instead of breaking any actual rules it was more a case of me forgetting things like common decency. Allow me to explain.

While at a big swimming gala in Wolverhampton one day I was standing in a room at the top of the building next to the scoreboard and quickly noticed that, whenever the scores went up, everyone down below looked up in unison. The room I was in had a viewing area and so, in addition to me being able to see the crowd, they could all see me. This gave me an idea. After the next race when the scores were about to go up I got as close to the scoreboard as I could. Then, about a second before the scores went up, I turned around and pulled a moonie. I might not have been able to see the reaction to me showing my arse to the great and the good of the West Midlands swimming fraternity (although I wish I could), but I could most certainly hear it and it was exactly as you'd expect.

Unfortunately for me and our team, the president of the Amateur Swimming Association was in town that day and within about ten minutes of me pulling down my trunks the entire team had been threatened with disqualification. Personally I thought that was a bit OTT but you know what these official types are like. No sense of humour! Fortunately for everyone concerned, my coach Arnold was as proficient in acts of diplomacy as he was recognising talent in the pool, so thanks to him disaster was averted. I still don't know how I would have reacted had the president of the ASA followed through with his threat because I'd always got away with being mischievous. It wouldn't have ended well though and knowing me I'd have either given him a repeat performance or turned around and shown him the other side. I had a habit of doing that too, I'm afraid.

The escapade that got the biggest laugh happened at another swimming gala and involved me borrowing a garment from a young lady. Whenever I made my way to the pool at a gala the first thing I did was look for my parents (all kids do it) but on this particular occasion I was keener than ever to spot them. This was because, unlike all the other competitors, I was wearing a bathrobe. When Mum and Dad saw me wearing it they looked absolutely terrified, and with good reason. They knew I was up to something but obviously had no idea what it was. Mum's told me later that her biggest fear was that I had nothing on underneath and when I was called onto the blocks she and Dad had already made their way to the aisle seats so they could make a quick getaway if need be.

When my name was eventually called out I slowly and provocatively undid the bathrobe to reveal that I was wearing Becky Dulson's swimsuit. Becky was a team mate of mine and because she had a spare swimsuit with her that day I had asked if I could borrow it. The entire place erupted when I finally took off the bathrobe but I don't think anybody was particularly surprised. I was famous for pulling stunts like that and I think that, like Mum, they were just relieved I wasn't bollock naked. That's still an ambition of mine, though. If you ever see me at a strongman event dressed in a bathrobe, run like fuck.

I kept the swimsuit on, by the way, and won the race easily, which probably prevented me from getting into trouble. It was just another normal day at the pool really.

Chapter 7

Talking of putting the wind up my parents, which I've actually turned into a bit of an art over the years, it was about this time that I got my nipple pierced and once again I chose to break it to them with as much drama as I could muster.

I'd already asked them both if I could have my ears pierced but they'd said I wasn't allowed until I was sixteen and had left school. As it turned out I ended up leaving school well before I was sixteen (or was I pushed? You'll find out soon enough), but even though I'd been banned from having my ears pierced, nobody ever said anything about nipples. It was quite fashionable then and so just for a laugh I got it done one day while I was out on the piss with some mates. It hurt like hell though! After that, at swimming, I'd had to wear a plaster over my nipple and Mum had asked me once or twice what was wrong. 'Oh, nothing,' I fibbed. 'I just caught it on something.' Well, I had caught it on something. A bloody piercing machine!

A few days later, Mum was in the kitchen on her own one afternoon and so before Dad got home I thought I'd break it to her so that she could tell him later on my behalf.

'Mum,' I said shiftily. 'You know you said I couldn't have my ears pierced?'

Once again, the look on Mum's face represented the horror of things to come, or things she *thought* were to come, and as I slowly began taking my T-shirt off she stood there looking at me through squinted eyes.

'What have you done?' she said. 'Please tell me it's not a tattoo!'

'It's worse than that,' I said, trying to wind her up even more.

Once the nipple ring was revealed, Mum let out groan. 'Oh my good God!' she said. 'Don't tell your dad. He'll go mad!'

As it turned out, Dad didn't go mad at all so it was all a bit of an anti-climax. They were obviously saving their outrage up for when I got my tattoos.

When Arnold and I eventually travelled to Ponds Forge in Sheffield for the 2001 Nationals I don't mind admitting that, inside at least, I was absolutely bricking it. I was still super-confident and shockingly arrogant but it was like going into the unknown and that was seriously daunting. Also, I don't think I'd ever been pitched against the best of the best in anything before and so this was the ultimate test for me. It was the ultimate test for everyone, I suppose.

It's no exaggeration to say that in order to get to the National finals you have to beat, or be better than, literally tens of thousands of kids and whoever ultimately triumphs is the best our country has to offer in their category and age group. That is one serious accolade when you think about it and fortunately for me the size of the prize far outweighed the anxiety I was feeling. Arnold also reminded me that everybody there would be anxious and that also made a difference. What made the biggest difference though was that I knew, in my heart of hearts, that I was the most talented swimmer in the building. Other people obviously didn't believe that but who cared what they thought? I believed it and Arnold believed it, and by the time I was called to the blocks for my first race I was ready to give my opponents the aquatic equivalent of a right good kicking.

Sure enough, an hour or so later I was the proud owner of four golds medals, a silver medal and two – count 'em – two new British records. The results were as follows:

50m freestyle, 26:43 – 1st

100m freestyle, 57:01 – 1st

200m freestyle, 2:04 – 2nd

400m freestyle, 4:19.02 – 1st

1500m freestyle, 17:31.86 – 1st

The only reason I didn't win the 200m is because my arm touched one of the ropes and that cost me about half a second. Otherwise, I'd have been able to keep my original promise to Mum and Dad and win the lot. Never mind, though. Four out of five wasn't bad for a first attempt, he said modestly.

At the time, I actually remember trying to blame Mum for the silver, but she wasn't having any of it. For breakfast that morning she'd given me something different to what I usually had and as a self-confessed creature of habit who found it hard to accept that he may have made a mistake, I pointed the finger at Mum's last-minute catering alteration. I forget exactly what she said to me but it definitely ended with 'off'.

Winning four golds and a silver at the same championship was as rare as rocking-horse shit but what was even more remarkable was that times I triumphed with were faster than many of the older age groups. The icing on the cake though, if my memory serves me correctly, was hearing that my time of 26:43 in the 50m had beaten the record held by Mark Foster. I'd beaten my hero. Actually, I think I'd thrashed him!

If I was a confident young lad going in to the 2001 Nationals, I was felt unconquerable coming out. I remember thinking to myself that every single piece of advice Arnold had given me, and everything I'd done to try and better myself, had now been vindicated. There's a photo in this book of me, Arnold and the medals and I never tire of looking at it. What an amazing day.

CHAPTER 8

Putting the Boot into Boot Camp

As is so often way, I soon became a victim of my own success and not long after triumphing at the 2001 Nationals I was selected for what was called the World Class Potential Programme. This was basically a residential boot camp that took place quarterly, which was attended by some of the country's finest young swimmers as well as top-notch coaches who had been flown in from all over the world. Coaches who were used to training Olympians, by the way, as opposed to over-confident, cross-dressing, moonie-pulling trouble-makers with Mohicans.

The person who was most pleased with me being picked for the World Class Potential Programme, apart from Mum and Dad, was Arnold, and that's completely understandable. To him it was the ultimate compliment – a kid he'd trained being earmarked for greatness – whereas to me it was the beginning of the end. From the very moment I enrolled on the programme I was given a new training regime that was to be implemented and overseen by Arnold and to say that I disagreed with the content of the programme would be a gross understatement. In all, I had to swim about 50,000 metres every week but instead of concentrating on swimming freestyle like you'd expect I was spending just as much time swimming backstroke, breast stroke and butterfly – none of which I really enjoyed and none of which were any use to me.

All of a sudden, everything had become very, very serious and business-like and once I began being annoyed by it, I very quickly began to hate it. I remember feeling gutted that things had changed and couldn't for the life of me understand why they'd had to go and spoil it all. Arnold and I had done unbelievably well up to now and we had medals and records to prove it. I obviously appreciate that changes would have to be made in order for me to progress, but because the modifications were so stark, and because it was all done in such a dull, militarised fashion, I decided to go to war.

One of the more light-hearted examples of my belligerence took place at Loughborough University during one of these boot camps and involved a swimming pool that had a viewing area underneath and to the sides, enabling the coaching staff to observe you swimming. Half way through a training session one day I decided to have a bit of fun. Dad was in attendance that morning, although not at the pool, and as the coaches all stood there waiting for me to pass I decided to whip off my trunks (yes, I know, again!) and give them something more interesting to observe. Unfortunately for Dad, the coaches always filmed these training sessions and an hour or so later he was called into one of the offices and shown a film of me basically skinny dipping. Obviously, that embarrassed him somewhat but at the time I couldn't have given two shits.

What upset me most about all this was that Arnold had become completely taken in by the new regime. Once again that's entirely understandable. To him, working with all these Olympic coaches was like hitting the big time but instead of him continuing to be his own man – and a very forceful and independent one at that – he just turned into a puppet for these Olympic pricks.

The boot camps themselves were all run with military precision We always got up at 5 a.m. and after a nice two-hour swim we'd have breakfast. After that we'd do gym work followed by something like yoga and then we'd break for lunch. The afternoons always started with a nice bit of body conditioning and to round off the day you'd have another two-hour swim. It was the same every day, by the way, and the discipline was as military in style as the precision. This, I'm afraid, is why things really started going belly-up. All I wanted to do when I turned up to one of these boot camps was get into a bloody fight. Not a physical fight, but a verbal one. Once again, I don't mind things like rules and discipline, providing you can convince me that they're all there for the greater good. This would have been unthinkable to the coaching staff because as far as they were concerned we were just commodities: teenage swimming machines who were there to work and do exactly as we were told.

They had this system where, if you were late for a training session or a meal or whatever, you were given a black tick and if you got three black ticks you were sent home. I was thirteen years of age when I entered this programme and you don't treat thirteen-year-olds like that, for Christ's sake. Or at least I don't think you should. First of all you earn the respect of the pupils, as Arnold had with me, and then, providing you do a good job of teaching them, you shouldn't need to enforce a load of demeaning and preposterous rules. Having a punishment system like that in place and then ramming it down people's throats all the time means that you're obviously expecting the worst from them and, in my case, that immediately put me on the back foot. Why not show a bit of trust first, and then, if someone does step out of line, have a quick word? It's not rocket science.

These big-time coaches didn't give a toss about my well-being or about who I was or what made me tick. All they cared about was me sticking to a training programme and abiding by the rules. To them I wasn't a human being. I was a potential medal winner who'd help them reach a target. Had I chosen to surrender my character and become one of their robots, the chances are I'd have made it to the Olympics. In fact, I know I would. To me, though, it wasn't worth the sacrifice. Instead of being the plucky self-starter who promised his parents he'd win at the Nationals, I'd have been part of some Olympic production line. Worst of all I'd have been betraying my true self and even if I had won a gold medal at the Olympics I'd have derived no satisfaction from it whatsoever. I really mean that. It doesn't matter how big the prize is, the most important thing is being true to yourself.

When it came to working with Arnold day to day I still went through the motions, but deep down inside I knew that it was all bollocks and so I no longer gave him 100 per cent. I just couldn't. He seemed to be a totally different person to me and thanks to the new training regime every ounce of enjoyment had been stripped away. As opposed to being passionate about my training, Arnold had become almost fanatical. The longer it went on the more distance there was between us.

This first started manifesting itself at the 2002 Nationals at Ponds Forge. I still came away with two golds but because I was now on the World Class Potential Programme and part of the junior elite I'd been expected to at least match last year's performance. The fact that I didn't pissed a lot of people off, not least Arnold. He obviously had to report back to the WCPP and as well as questioning my commitment and ability they may well have questioned his, too.

Unsurprisingly, this resulted in a series of arguments between Arnold and me and as I became more and more uninterested in proceedings, and as Arnold became more frustrated, the arguments got worse.

At the end of a training session Arnold would say, 'Why are you pissing about, Ed? What the hell's up with you?' And I'd reply, 'Well, what the hell's up with you? You've completely changed, Arnold!' It was petty crap really.

One day the inevitable happened and it all came to a head. It was at the end of an afternoon session and after receiving yet another one of Arnold's rollockings I said something I perhaps shouldn't have and then after Arnold had done the same I told him this was no longer for me. The following day I changed swimming clubs from Newcastle to COSACCS, which stands for the City of Stoke on Trent Swimming Club, although you'd never know from the initials! From my first session with COSACCS I immediately fell in love with swimming all over again. The atmosphere was so relaxed and everybody seemed happy.

Me leaving Newcastle was a big kick in the teeth for Arnold as I was obviously his star pupil and even today I feel sorry about the way it ended. If it isn't broken, though, why mend it? Modify it, if you have to, but by making it unrecognisable I'd forgotten where the initial success came from and once that had happened, I was gone.

My coach at COSSACS was a man called Greg Clark, who is still in charge there, and although I never got my edge back in the pool he allowed me to be myself and we had an excellent working relationship. He understood that trying to change me would only ever lead to trouble and he told me that apparently Mark Foster had had a very similar personality. The difference between Mark and me, though, is that there was evidently a limit to his intransigence; where he was prepared to make certain compromises in order to succeed, I was not. In fact, looking back, the only compromise I made during my swimming career was taking my foot off the gas so I could start enjoying the sport again, so in that respect it made me the worst possible kind of competitor.

At about the same time as Arnold and I parted ways I decided to say a fond farewell to the World Class Potential Programme. This was going to be fun.

The person in charge of the World Class Potential Programme was an Australian man called Bill Sweetenham and it's safe to say that he and I never really got on. He was the National Performance Director for the Great Britain swimming team from 2000 till 2007 and he was head of the Argentinian national swimming team for several years until 2014. He was the one who'd come up with all that black tick bollocks and I couldn't stand the man. To me he was the reason I no longer enjoyed swimming and I'd been itching to tell him what I thought of him since the off.

This opportunity to press my self-destruct button eventually arose at one of the boot camps. As usual, not long after we arrived, one of Sweetenham's lackeys came around and gave us all the 'three black ticks and you're out' lecture. There were no words of welcome or encouragement, just threats of what would happen if we didn't toe the line.

After having this read to us yet again something inside me clicked and I thought to myself, *Naah, this isn't for me.* As *far as I'm concerned you can all go and fuck yourselves.* The button had now been pressed and there was no turning back.

Although some of the other kids there were OK they were all quite posh and so I didn't really click with any of them. On top of that they were all good little boys and girls who'd obviously been beaten into submission and to tell the truth I just felt sorry for them. Being a promising swimmer back then was a very, very miserable existence.

My first act of defiance took place in the hotel we were staying at but the results far exceeded my expectations. I'd decided to spark up a cigarette in my room, knowing full well that somebody would tell the coaches, but instead of hearing a knock at the door and receiving a black tick an alarm went off and the entire hotel had to be evacuated. I remember standing in the car park surrounded by hundreds of people thinking gleefully, *I am in so much fucking trouble!*

Not surprisingly, Sweetenham and his coaching monkeys went absolutely apeshit and so within hours of arriving I'd already been given two black ticks. Two! Why I wasn't sent home there and then amazes me but not long after being given the ticks I had another knock at my door. 'Mr Sweetenham would like to see you in his hotel room now,' said a very stern-looking coach. This was my big opportunity.

'I'll tell you what,' I said. 'Tell that fat twat that he can come and see me.'

Five minutes later I was no longer a member of the World Class Potential Programme and had been removed indefinitely from Mr Sweetenham's Christmas card list. It was sad that it had to end that way but I'd far sooner get kicked out for calling the man who'd spoilt it all a twat than have my parents write him a letter. There was no way I was just going to leave that programme voluntarily. I had to be given the boot.

But before we move on from swimming I just wanted to tell you about one of the more enjoyable experiences I had in a pool, which happened just after my fourteenth birthday. I could have left it with me calling Sweetenham a twat but over the years I've had far more good times than bad in the water and I think I need to emphasise that and not leave the subject on a downer. Incidentally, if there are any budding strength athletes reading this who don't currently swim, then take my advice and do it. The benefits it will have, not just on your performance but on your health in general, are many and varied and if I hadn't had it as a platform there's no way I'd be where I am today. Just make sure you wear the right costume and if anyone tries to piss around with your training routine tell them to do one.

Anyway, back to my happy swimming memory. I'm not sure if it still happens today but every March at Fenton Manor Pool in Stoke they used to hold a 5k swimathon to raise money for charity. If memory serves me correctly it was all part of something national and a few weeks after it had taken place the people with the best times in each category were all invited to a dinner and a presentation. I have no idea how many people took part in the swimathon countrywide, but as it was such a massive event there must have been hundreds or maybe thousands in each category. Because I was back in love with the sport (although not for long), I was well up for it. I didn't train for that distance but I was as fit as a butcher's dog and knew I was more than a match for it.

The time I eventually posted in the thirteen to fifteen age category was one hour, one minute and fifteen seconds and at the risk of sounding like a big-head I completely annihilated the rest of the country. Seriously, that's quick. No other child came close to that time and I'm pretty sure it was the fastest overall. According to one or two swimming websites a 5k swim should take most fitness swimmers between ninety minutes and two hours so that gives you a good idea of how fast it was.

The gala dinner and presentation was held at Butlin's in Minehead and we – as in me, Mum and Dad – had an all-expenses-paid weekend there. I'd never been able to take my parents anywhere before and so being able to treat them was fantastic. Better still, it didn't cost me a penny!

On the Saturday night the Butlin's Redcoats started off proceedings with a big show and then after dinner Duncan Goodhew presented all the awards. I got a photo, of course, which pleased me no end, but it was only at the dinner that I realised how big a deal it was and that made it better still. It was a very proud moment.

One of the primary reasons I wanted to do well at the 5k swimathon was because, just a few weeks previously, my nan had been diagnosed with acute lymphoblastic leukaemia. She was very ill when she started treatment and in all kinds of pain.

This was the first time in my young life that I'd had to deal with the prospect of losing somebody dear to me and the fact that it was Nan made it especially hard to bear. She could always bring out the best in me no matter what the situation, for the simple reason that I knew how much she loved me. Because of this, and because of the amount of pain she was in, I desperately wanted to take Nan's mind off things and at the same time make her proud of me. I knew I could be a pain in the arse sometimes and so wanted to compensate her. I seem to have a habit of doing that!

I think it worked, though, and when Nan found out that I'd won the swimathon she was in floods of tears, and because she was in floods of tears, so was I. Unfortunately Nan was too ill to come to the presentation, but even so, she knew I'd done it for her and that meant everything to me.

CHAPTER 9

Losing My Way (and Finding It)

Despite the successful swimathon, Nan's diagnosis hit me harder than I originally thought and marked the start of what was a difficult couple of years. The worst, in fact. By this point the swimming was starting to go tits up and with that on the wane and Nan being ill I'm afraid I started reverting to my former self. Or should I say, a version of my former self. I was a couple of years older now and instead of just fighting and smoking weed I was now drinking booze like it was going out of fashion and this took the fighting element to a completely different level.

My brothers will bear witness to this but when I started going off the rails I could drink a full bottle of whisky in a single night, no problem. Sometimes more. Because I was so fit, and because I was also a big lad, it didn't affect me as much as it would most people and so in order to get completely off my face and forget about everything I had to down stupid amounts. That was why I did it, because I wanted to block out Nan's diagnosis, and it worked an absolute treat. I'd drink and then slowly but surely everything would seem OK. For a time. The real problem was the volume of sprits I was drinking, and I'm not just talking about the alcoholic volume, although that was definitely a contributing factor. You see, the more I drank the higher my tolerance became and the higher my tolerance became the more I drank. The result of this vicious intoxicating circle was more violence and after a while all I wanted to do was hurt people. For a time I became a seriously fucked-up individual (some people would say I still am!) and, as well as inducing in me some pretty serious bouts of depression and anxiety, the situation also led to some serious injuries.

Probably the worst of these happened about halfway through 2002 and the reason for the fight, I'm now very ashamed to say, was a pair of my brother's stinking trainers. The other person involved was an eighteen-year-old guy who lived near us. He'd nicked my brother's trainers from our doorstep one day and then a few nights later while I was out on the lash he turned up and started bragging about it. 'Hey, your lad's trainers are comfortable,' he laughed, and I remember saying, or slurring, 'Piss off, you creepy fucker.' By this point I'd already had well over a bottle of scotch and although my alcohol tolerance level was high I was now barely able to stand up. Even so, I still offered to fight the weirdo but instead of jumping up and giving him a kicking like I would have if I were sober, I just fell back on my arse. I was bolloxed.

Now I don't remember any of this but this dickhead obviously saw an opportunity while I was drunk and so as I was sitting there out of my head he took a run-up and kicked me full-on in the face. To this day, and this is God's honest truth, he is the only person who has ever got the better of me in a fight and I had to be battered for it to happen.

If somebody takes a run-up at you and toe-punts you in the face – even a soft-arsed prick like that – it's going to make a mess. Sure enough, my face was now far from perfect and as well as having a very badly broken nose, which had to be reconstructed, I also had to have endoscopic sinus surgery so that I could breathe properly. Mum and Dad were not happy, but then I wasn't exactly over the moon. I'd been a pretty good-looking lad until then and for a while afterwards I looked like the Elephant Man.

The one positive thing to come out of 2002 (apart from the swimathon), and it's a pretty significant one when you think about it, was that it was the year I first joined a gym, and no prizes for guessing who my inspiration was. Step right up, Mr Arnold Schwarzenegger. You remember the scene in *The Terminator* sequel when he walks up to those dickheads and says, 'I need your clothes, your boots and your motorcycle.' Well, I was watching that one day when all of a sudden I thought, *I could look like that if I put my mind to it*. This was a genuine defining moment for me and once again I gathered my parents around me so I could announce my intentions.

'Mum, Dad,' I said. 'I'm going to have a body like Arnold Schwarzenegger.' I think I said previously that Mum and Dad never once derided my ambitions and whenever I told them something like this they'd just nod and say, 'OK, son. You'd better crack on with it then.'

The gym I joined was Total Fitness and even though I was fourteen and you weren't supposed to lift weights until you were eighteen I still managed to blag my way in. This was something I became an expert at in my teens. I definitely looked a lot older than I was and because I was tall and broad the gym owners assumed I knew what I was doing. And I did, to a certain extent, because I'd seen people train before. But anything I didn't know I just picked up while I was there. I seemed to click more with adults than I did with kids and everyone was very helpful. Just to put my size into perspective, Dad was about six foot two inches and fourteen stone at the time and I was an inch shorter but the same weight. From the word go I behaved, looked and trained like a fully grown adult and pretty soon I was lifting weights like one. Everything was in place: I had a super-strong heart, a massive lung capacity and there wasn't an ounce of fat on me, and because I was also quite young I put muscle on very easily. I was just built for it.

From a mental point of view this was exactly what I needed and so I gave it my all. You already know there are no half measures with me but going to the gym gave me a purpose in life, and with things like swimming going tits up and school about to do the same I needed a purpose more than ever.

Ah yes, my education. I was hoping you'd forgotten about that.

CHAPTER 10

Downhill to Expulsion

As life outside of school began to deteriorate after Nan's diagnosis, life inside school followed pretty much the same path. It was a mixture, really, of fights, detentions, isolations, suspensions, lunchtime spliffs and lots and lots of bad language. The majority of the isolations and detentions came from telling teachers to fuck off and the suspensions usually resulted from fights. I'd fight anybody, regardless of year, and slowly but surely I helped to create an epidemic. I'm getting a feeling of déjà vu here. Are you? Some of the stuff we did you'd go to prison for these days but back then you could get away with a lot at high school. Or at least you could at ours. I'm certainly not proud of it. In fact, I'm completely and utterly ashamed and always cite my behaviour at school as being the benchmark of how not to live your life.

The environment, as I've already said, wasn't really conducive to getting a good education but I'd already proved that I could rise above that and so the only person to blame for things going tits up was me. I really was a complete dickhead, to be honest, and if I'd been the headmaster I'd have fired me into fucking space. As it was, they only fired me as far as home but it was enough to rid the school of one of its most troublesome pupils.

I was so, so angry though. That is the all-pervading emotion I remember feeling back then and it was as if I'd become possessed. I was the original Mr Angry! When you wake up in the morning the first thing you do is look at the clock, right? Well, when I woke up, the first thing I did was experience a sudden rush of anger and to stop it getting worse I'd have to lie in bed for a few minutes. The worst bit was feeling the veins on the side of my head throbbing and sometimes I honestly thought my head was going to explode. It was terrifying. The more I wanted it to go away, the angrier and more frustrated I became. It was yet another vicious circle.

Nan's diagnosis was definitely the catalyst for my fury but the alcohol and everything else made it much worse. Looking back it was like a series of unfortunate events, culminating in my expulsion from school. First Nan was diagnosed, then the swimming started going belly up. After that I started drinking, which is when the depression and anxiety appeared, and once I started fighting again all hope was lost.

By the way, I should say that Mum and Dad had absolutely no idea that all this was going on. They know now, of course, and they knew about the suspensions from school and the depression; but as far as all the drinking and a lot of the fighting were concerned, they were completely unaware. This isn't because they were bad parents, by the way. Anything but. It's because, like most people with problems or addictions, I became very adept at hiding them and when I eventually told Mum and Dad what had been going on they were flabbergasted. And upset, it has to be said.

The depression and anxiety would stay with me until my late teens, and you might be surprised when I tell you what finally released me from it. But like a lot of things in my life, it was something I felt I had to deal with on my own (I did take Prozac for a while but it made me feel worse) and for a lad in his mid-teens with more issues than a soap opera, that was no mean feat. The anxiety was crippling at times. I would be assailed by an overwhelming feeling that everything in my life was going wrong, and because there was so much backing up the idea that this was actually the case, the anxiety very quickly span out of control.

The depression, though. That was something far more disturbing. It first started manifesting itself when I began having thoughts about being shit and worthless. Fairly textbook, I suppose. Then, as they became a regular fixture, I started having thoughts about killing myself. Sometimes I could barely move it was so bad and I've never cried so much in my entire life. Whenever I thought about my nan a feeling of desperation would hit me like a truck. Then, as that began to subside, sadness would take over. That's when the crying would start, followed by the suicidal thoughts. Third in line would be anger and after that it would be booze, fights and trouble.

Just when I thought that things couldn't get any worse I went out one night, got pissed, pulled a girl and ended up getting her pregnant. What an absolute twat! When she told me I was completely devastated and it amplified the depression and anxiety ten-fold. All I did during this time was cry, drink and fight, and as far as my thinking mind was concerned any hopes of me having a bright future had disappeared. Gone forever, and all because of a drunken shag.

Eventually both mine and the girl's families met up and it was decided that the best thing for everyone concerned would be a termination. It's not my proudest moment by any stretch of the imagination but because of where I was at the time mentally and what it might have done to me had it gone ahead, it was definitely the right thing to do. More importantly, though, the girl involved was only my age and far too young to become a mother.

The relief I felt once that was sorted out was deep and it actually gave me a platform to recover, although only a very small one. In any case, because of my self-belief, and maybe even my narcissism, I never took the suicidal thoughts seriously enough to act on them. Deep down I guess I always knew there was hope. Come on, what would the world do without me, for heaven's sake? I don't mind admitting, though, that the depression and anxiety absolutely flattened me and if I hadn't had that intrinsic self-belief bubbling away underneath all the alcohol and the suicidal thoughts I might well have ended up travelling to a much darker place. Thank God I'm a bighead!

Chapter 10

Anyway, I know you're dying to find out how I got expelled, so without any further ado, let's crack on.

There was this lad at school. I can't really tell you what he's called but even his name still makes my temples twitch! Although he was as big as me he was a right flabby fucker and I absolutely detested him, and him me. There were two reasons for this: first, he was a massive bully and used to go around smacking up geeks, and second, we were seen as the two hardest lads in the school, and as you know I do not like sharing titles. It was the bullying that used to piss me off the most. I'm not saying I was perfect by any means, but I would only ever fight people who were up for it or who mouthed off and I certainly didn't go around attacking geeks. The lad was a complete coward and if there's one thing I hate more than flabby fuckers who think they're hard, it's flabby fuckers who attack geeks. It's not on, pal!

The longer this went on, the more I wanted to hurt this prick. So eventually I devised a plan where I could get him on his own and teach him a lesson.

It was snowing at the time and the plan was for one of my mates to throw a snowball at this lads and then run off into the woods. Sensing an opportunity to hit somebody smaller than him, he would then follow my mate, hoping to catch him. Ha, ha! No chance. Once he was in the woods I would then appear from behind a tree and challenge him to a scrap. Easy really.

These sorts of things don't always go according to plan but on this particular occasion it went like a dream. Or a nightmare, for one flabby fucker. My mate threw the snowball at this lad and hit him on the back on the head. He then chased my mate into the woods, I appeared and, *voilà*, one scrap waiting to happen. I was so up for this fight it was unreal and after about twenty seconds it all came to an end when I headbutted him and knocked his front teeth out. My only regret was that he didn't put up more of a fight but despite our similarity in size he was wheezing like an asthmatic after a few seconds.

Although the fight took place outside the school it was during the lunch break and so still deemed as being in school time. This meant that one of the first people to hear about it was the headmaster. I knew what was going to happen; it was the final straw. Sure enough, the following day my parents were informed that I'd been expelled and, in a way, I think they were relieved. I certainly was. Mum and Dad knew I had problems and to be honest my head was like a fucking hamster's wheel at that time. The noise was non-stop! In order to complete my GCSEs and not end up in borstal I needed the least number of distractions as possible, not to mention fewer fellow fifteen-year-olds, and so expulsion was actually the best thing for me and definitely the best thing for the school. In fact, I bet they got the bunting out when I walked through the gates for the last time.

As soon as I was expelled from school, some home tuition was arranged and from then until the end of Year Eleven I was basically left to my own devices. I didn't take the piss, though, and when I wasn't being tutored I was usually down the gym. A lot of people assume that home tuition is something either tree huggers or posh people use for their kids, but in the Stoke area circa 2003 it was a luxury reserved mainly for kids who had either been expelled or for kids who had serious issues. Kids like me, basically!

In fact the home tuition worked really well for me and I ended up getting better GCSE grades than any of my friends at school. This was partly down to my tutor, Keith. He's one of that select band of adults I told you about who managed to influence me, and without him I'm not sure I'd have done half as well as I did.

If my parents were around, Keith would come to our house to tutor me but if they weren't we'd have to meet somewhere public. Bearing in mind the kind of kids they were tutoring this rule was probably put in place to protect the tutors rather than the pupils and whenever I did meet Keith in a public place this theory was pretty much borne out. I'd always turn up early which meant I'd see Keith with the pupils he had prior to me and over the months I saw him get screamed at, kicked, punched and spat on. How the hell he put up with it all is something I will never be able to fathom but by the time I sat down he was calm and ready to go. Most people would have murdered the little bastards, and from what I could see they'd have been doing the world a favour.

Because I liked Keith I had no problem working for him, and after seeing him being abused like that I wanted to give the man a break. But it was how he treated me that had the biggest effect and, a bit like that supply teacher, he genuinely seemed to care. Keith obviously knew the background of why I'd been expelled but he never judged me and he never held it against me. What he did do, apart from getting me through my GCSEs, was to say things that rejuvenated me and made me feel positive about the future.

One day after a lesson he said, 'Do you know, Eddie, you're totally different to the other kids I teach. You're polite, well behaved and you've got a brain. You may have a few issues but I have no doubt whatsoever that you will overcome these and become a success.'

I must have had a seventy-four-inch chest after he said that, at least! This wasn't just a script though, or if it was he was a bloody good actor. Keith knew full well that the direction of my life was in the balance and he wanted to do everything he possibly could to push me the right way. I have no doubt whatsoever that he'd have tried doing the same with all the other kids but I also know that, in many cases, he'd have been fighting a losing battle. Kids like me – the ones who were redeemable – were probably the reason he got out of bed in the morning and there was no fucking way I was going to let him down.

CHAPTER 11
Twenty Police, Two Brothers

Thanks to Keith, and a bit of hard work, I came away from full-time education with seven A–C-grade GCSEs including an A in Physical Education and a B in Maths. I hadn't suddenly become a budding academic or a paragon of virtue, but I was now a proud, well-balanced and reasonably well-educated young man who, after some extremely trying times, had gone some way to repaying the efforts of a handful of incredibly special adults: Mum, Dad, Nan, Mrs Mills, Mr Stirland, Keith (sorry for not remembering your surname, Keith), and the supply teacher whose name also unfortunately escapes me. It's all very well having faith in yourself, but having the faith of people you respect and/or love is the umbrella under which it all sits.

By the time I took my GCSEs you could easily have mistaken me for a thirty-year-old man. I was about six foot two inches, sixteen stone, and I had a skinhead, a pierced nipple and scars all over me. I looked as rough as a nut! But because of what had happened over the last couple of years I also had both the personality and the character to match my mature appearance and looking back I definitely benefited from all that independence. Who cares if it was enforced?

Two other things I benefited from back then, and do now, were my parents' work ethic, which has always been impressive, and a morbid fear of being skint. The latter had been with me since high school and – coupled with an entrepreneurial spirit, a bit of nous and a few decent contacts – I took more money from my fellow pupils than the lady working the till in the dinner hall.

I started off by selling cigarettes, which were easy to get hold of, and I'd sell one for 50p. Bearing in mind they were probably about £3 a pack back then that's not a bad mark-up and right from Year Seven I was like a walking tobacconist. 'Two Lambert & Butler? Yeah, OK. That's a quid. Go on then, piss off.' I was like a cross between Del Boy and Charles Bronson.

Once the entrepreneur in me had started coming to the fore I moved on to selling dodgy PlayStation games and was chipping consoles left right and centre. After that I started selling pirate DVDs. In my four and a bit years at high school I must have made thousands.

Despite all the crap going on in my life, this made me realise that there were very few people in the world who were willing, or able, to be the ones who would provide the products and services needed in whatever environment you were in. As well as opening my eyes, it helped me to spot the opportunities.

Now I was out in the big wide world these qualities would be just what I needed and they'd start coming into play in about a year; or, in the case of this book, a page or two. In the meantime, I decided to enrol on a three-year course in electrical engineering at the local college. I'm not entirely sure why I chose electrical engineering, apart from having a vague interest in the subject, and I was planning to explore how I'd use the qualification as I progressed. I had one or two ideas in my head but to be honest the whole thing was a compromise really. I had to do something.

After about three weeks of being a budding electrical engineer I started to lose interest and as well as being bored shitless I could feel the walls closing in around me. There was certainly more freedom at the college than there had been at high school but everything else was the same and pretty soon I hated it. I think I lasted three months in all but by the end I was literally banging the doors down. I felt like I'd been re-institutionalised and I promised myself then that I would never, ever darken the door of full-time education again. I could get by without it, and it could certainly get by without me.

By this point I was hitting the gym quite hard and as I started lifting more, I obviously started eating more and using things like protein supplements, and, as many of you know, these don't come cheap. I hated being dependent on anybody, least of all Mum and Dad, and so I needed to find some money quickly.

Luckily, Mum saw an advert in a local paper one day advertising for an apprentice truck mechanic in a place called Cobridge, and so straightaway I applied. There were two apprenticeships up for grabs, and there were about fifteen applicants in all. This was the first time I'd ever been to a job interview, and although it's not something I particularly enjoyed I felt like it had gone well. I've always had a knack of being able to get on somebody's wavelength pretty quickly. You could put the most boring prat in the world in front of me and I guarantee that within five minutes I'll have found out what makes them tick and will be telling them jokes about stamp collecting or whatever.

I came away from that apprenticeship interview with a bit of a spring in my step and when Mum asked me how it had gone I informed her that I was more than quietly confident. I treated it like a competition, which I suppose it was, and despite not being desperate to become a truck mechanic, I desperately wanted to beat the other applicants. A few days later I received a letter telling me I'd done just that, so a week or two after that I finally made my debut in the world of legitimate employment as an apprentice HGV mechanic at LEX Commercial, Cobridge. It was never going to make me a millionaire but I ended up enjoying it: it was mentally and physically challenging enough to keep me interested and got me used to a routine. With overtime, I'd sometimes work up to fifty hours a week and with the twenty or so I spent in the gym that left little time for socialising. This was actually a godsend, as when I did find time to go out it nearly always ended in – yes, you guessed it – trouble.

As with my transgressions at the swimming boot camps, I could offer you dozens of cringe-worthy examples of my less-than perfect behaviour on the streets of Stoke, but for my mum's sake I'm just going to stick with the one. It's a bloody good one though.

I was still sixteen at the time and because I hadn't been out in a while my brother James suggested that we go out on the piss together. Bearing in mind our temperaments, this probably wasn't the wisest of proposals and we ended up taking on half the Stoke constabulary. We actually did OK, as it goes.

Up until about two in the morning we'd had a really good laugh and hadn't had a sniff of trouble all night. Then, as we were standing outside a nightclub, this bird, who was absolutely shitfaced, started gobbing off at James and calling him all kinds of shit. We'd both had a few and because this woman was three sheets to the wind we just told her to shut the fuck up. Unfortunately, she decided to ignore our advice and after another ten minutes or so of listening to her gobbing off, James and I started giving her some back. She looked a right state so we had plenty of ammunition.

Anyway, as we were all exchanging pleasantries an officer of the law stepped up and tried to intervene. At first I was relieved because I thought he might shut her up but instead of telling her to do one he started having a pop at James.

Whether or not this policeman was related to the woman I'm not sure, but she was evidently a lot more pissed than we were and also a damn sight more aggressive, so if anyone should have been reprimanded, it was her. This, I'm afraid to say, is when the fierier side of our temperaments started pushing themselves to the fore and before you could say 'somebody put a bag over this no-mark's head' we were surrounded by police officers.

Remember ages ago I talked about me, James and Alex being like miniature caged beasts whenever Mum put us in separate rooms? Well, as well as being caged once again we were now much, much bigger and as well as having about fifteen pints swilling around inside us we were getting really fucked off. Even though this woman was still swearing her arse off and trying to goad James, she still hadn't even been told to shut up by the police. We, on the other hand, were surrounded by about ten of them and every time James or I swore back at this gobby woman we were threatened with arrest.

'Hang on a second,' I said. 'She's has just called you a twat and you don't even bat an eyelid. What the fucking hell's up with you?'

'Swear like that once more, sir,' said the copper, 'and we'll lock you up.'

Never mind the woman goading us. The police were doing a far better job!

In the end, we'd had enough and so after being threatened again with arrest while this woman just carried on swearing and what have you, we told the police that they could fuck right off.

This was obviously exactly what they'd had been trying to engineer, and with a few lads egging us on from the pavement we readied ourselves for a bit of a ruck. James must have been about twenty-two stone at the time and because it was late in the year I'd have been touching seventeen. The police must have known we weren't going to come quietly so why the fuck they wound us up like that I have no idea. They must have fancied us.

After we'd sworn at them one of them stepped forward and tried to arrest James but as he did I grabbed him, threw him across the road and told him to fuck off. By this time all you could see were police officers and all you could hear were sirens. If you'd only just arrived in the area you'd have been forgiven for thinking there was a full-blown riot taking place.

For the next ten minutes or so small groups of police would move in and try to arrest us and every time they did we'd push them away or pick them up and chuck them into the road. It was a bit like a game you'd play at Cubs, but with a tiny bit more violence and more flashing lights. May the good Lord forgive me but it was absolutely fucking excellent. It also shut that woman up, which was a bonus.

Eventually the police got fed up with being pushed and thrown, which was a shame, and so split into two groups;

one for me and one for James. Then, once they'd got themselves ready, they charged at us and began the unenviable task of trying to restrain us. According to one or two mates who witnessed the fracas it was pretty spectacular and it took about fifteen minutes for them to get us handcuffed and into the van.

Incidentally, the reason I sound so casual about what happened isn't because I don't have any respect for law and order. It's because I didn't like the way we were treated by the police and in my opinion they set out to get a reaction. All we did was stand up for ourselves and not let them shit on us, so yes, I quite enjoyed it.

A few weeks later James and I were up in court and got a reprimand. For as long as I live I will never forget what the judge said to us. He said:

'James and Edward Hall. What you did was not big and it certainly was not clever. You do realise it took over twenty police officers to restrain you? I for one don't think that's very impressive.'

I remember standing there grinning to myself, thinking, *I fucking do!* Twenty's an incredible number. Don't get me wrong, I certainly wasn't proud of getting arrested. I was just impressed by the way it happened.

CHAPTER 12

Getting Back on Track

By the time I was seventeen I'd cleaned up my act a bit and although I was hitting the gym harder than ever I still had no ambitions to become a strongman. Since being expelled I'd gradually cut out the drinking and, not surprisingly, this had had a positive effect on my depression. It was still there, but with my self-esteem making a comeback it had far less to go at.

The reason I was pushing harder gym, apart from wanting to look like Arnie, was the fact that I'd started doing some door work and I wanted to look as big and imposing as humanly possible. Actually, I think I'd always wanted to look as big as humanly possible but this gave me an excuse.

Even then, I knew that I was easily the strongest man in my gym and probably in the entire area. This was a big boost for me confidence-wise – a powerful realisation – and made me feel similar to how I feel when I win a strongman competition. I'll let you choose which one.

Some of you might be wondering how I knew that I was the strongest man in Stoke when I was just seventeen, and as a man who likes to back up his claims I'll be only too happy to tell you.

The first time I ever did a max bench press, which I did at seventeen, I pressed 180kg (397 lb) and my first ever max squat was a quarter of a tonne, or 250kg (551 lb). Not too shabby. My first ever max deadlift, which is obviously what I'm most famous for and took place at the same time, was 260kg (573 lb), which is over half the current world record held by that bearded bloke with the Mohican. Suave bastard.

Even today, I can count on the fingers of one hand the amount of people who can deadlift over 200kg (441 lb) at my gym, never mind 260kg. Anything over 200kg is a big deal if you're into lifting weights and so maxing 260kg on debut was fucking unbelievable.

Whilst I may not have been able to dedicate as much time to the gym as I did to my two jobs – that simply wasn't possible – I definitely spent more time thinking about it and the more I thought, the more I researched, and the more I was able to hone what I was doing and improve. I was also no slouch when it came to asking for advice and being surrounded by so many older and more experienced people was a big advantage. One of my very first gym partners was a local man in his forties who was a bodybuilder and powerlifter. He'd been training since before I was born and was obviously full of good advice. I was like a sponge in that respect and just soaked it all up.

The reason I started doing door work was because I was always skint and this was in small part down to all the money

I was spending on things like extra food, supplements, gym membership and equipment. Even then I was probably shelling out a good £80 a week on extra food and the same again on supplements. It doesn't take a mathematician to work out that a lad taking home about a grand a month won't have much left after spending that kind of money. So despite the fact that there weren't that many hours left in the day I thought I'd try to make the few that there were supplement my supplements, so to speak. Scraping by was never going be enough for me and I always needed to feel like I was progressing in life.

Yet again I wasn't really supposed to be working as a doorman at seventeen (you had to be at least eighteen) but because of my size and my character I got away with it. After blagging my way on to a door supervision course I started off working as an in-house doorman at several nightclubs four or five nights a week.

As well as extra money, the door work provided me with a bit of a social life and not being able to drink on the job meant it never interfered with the gym or with my apprenticeship. I was a bit tired sometimes the following day but at that age it doesn't matter. Don't worry, I hadn't turned into a complete teetotaller. I just drank occasionally.

I remember seeing all my friends from high school turn up to these nightclubs on a Friday and Saturday night and I'd watch them blow all their money and get completely off their heads. This used to happen week after week after week and it reinforced my desire to better myself, both physically and fiscally. I used to think, *Why would you do that to yourself? Why would you blow all your fucking money in one night?* It felt to me that as everyone else was going backwards, or at best treading water, I was moving forwards. The only things I ever had on a Sunday morning were a clear head and a bulging bank balance. To me that was very, very satisfying and was all the confirmation I needed that I was doing the right thing. I actually became a bit of a paragon of virtue for a while and whenever I got talking to friends who were in that 'work, get fucked and become skint' rut, I'd try to tell them, without sounding too pious, that there was an alternative. Nobody ever listened. Rather sadly, they ended up becoming my motivation because their apathy and stagnation used to scare the living shit out of me. The wider the gap between us, the better.

After working in-house at these clubs for few months I started becoming annoyed by the fact that it was always me who had to sort out things like cover for people who couldn't be arsed to turn up. I didn't ask for this responsibility, by the way, it just happened. I was reliable and always very professional so I was treated like a head doorman. This got me thinking that as opposed to doing it for free, maybe I should set up my own company, and that's what I did. I charged the venues so much per week and instead of doing it as a favour I shouldered all the hassle officially and got paid for it. It's bizarre, when you think about it. At seventeen years of age I was breaking up fights, throwing out drunks and telling groups of rowdy women to behave themselves. Then, just a few months later, I was employing a load of men twice my age and running the door of the majority of nightclubs in Stoke. If any of the doormen ever put a foot out of line I'd bollock them but I was always considered to be a very fair boss and never had much trouble. Every Friday night I'd visit all the clubs to give the men their wages and because they were self-employed and paid their own taxes I had bugger-all paperwork to deal with. It was easy really. But once again somebody had to come up with the idea and on this occasion, it was me.

One of the most amusing things about this situation, certainly given my age and also my past, was that in addition to liaising with the venue owners on an almost daily basis, who were all two or three times my age, I also had to liaise with the police about local troublemakers. Fortunately, none of them seemed to recognise me so it never became an issue but I remember thinking on several occasions while I was talking to them, *I'm sure I threw you into a road once.*

Despite the temptation, and I *was* tempted to say something, I was never unprofessional with any of the people I worked with and with some damn good money coming in (I must have been the wealthiest seventeen-year-old in Stoke), I was now able to splash out on some of the finer things in life, including a nice black BMW 3-series. I'd passed my driving test not long after my seventeenth birthday and managed to keep the BMW an entire four months before writing it off. It happened not long before my eighteenth birthday and was the first time I'd ever driven in icy conditions. Naturally, I was your archetypal boy racer so I saw ice more as an accelerant than a hazard and no allowances were made. This went quite well for the first couple of days but after channelling Ayrton Senna one afternoon I completely misjudged a roundabout, drove straight over it and then wrapped the car around a lamp post. It was like the time I fell out of that tree all those years ago. I'd almost killed myself yet all I could do was laugh. The rush was amazing!

Because my insurance was about £1,500 I didn't bother claiming on it and bought a clapped-out Fiesta just to get around in. It didn't have the same performance as the BMW but it was a hell of a lot safer.

Unfortunately, my addiction to speed was never going to be quashed by a prang in a Beamer and not too long after that I developed a passion for quad bikes. The first one I bought was a bog-standard Yamaha 250cc and after ripping the engine out I replaced it with a GSXR 600 from a superbike and stuck a turbo on it from a Subaru Impreza. Mark my words, this thing was fucking evil and because it had about 225 brake horsepower on the dyno I had to put drag swing arms on it to stop it wheeling, which it did in every gear. It also had racing suspension, racing tyres, racing brakes and everything was chrome dipped. It looked the absolute dog's bollocks and all in all I must have spent about £15,000 on it. It was my pride and joy.

Despite having laughed in the face of death one or twice up till then this quad bike was in a different league: it put me right inside its mouth and halfway down its fucking throat. It was just ridiculous. One day I got home after a near-miss that almost killed me and thought, *If I carry on driving that thing I'll be dead in a week.* You can't drive something like that slowly. It's all or nothing. And there was no way in the world I was going to fanny around in it at 30mph. That'd be like hiring a big bastard like me to move fucking pencils. No, it had to go unfortunately so that evening I put it on Ebay. Let it kill some other fucker!

I kind of made light of it before but I was working some unbelievable hours back then. For starters, my apprenticeship took up at least fifty hours a week (sometimes more if I had to work weekends) and my door work was at least another twenty. Add to that the twenty I spent training and you've got the best part of a hundred-hour week. I know they say that all work and no play makes Jack a dull boy but I absolutely loved it. I loved my day job, I loved being financially sound, I loved the social life that the gym and the door work gave me, and I loved the status they gave me too. I was the strongest bloke in the gym and I was the man who ran the doors in the nightclubs. It was exactly where any self-respecting young alpha male would want to be.

Even Nan seemed to perk up a bit for a while. Since being expelled we'd spent a lot of time together and despite being tired a lot of the time I think she was buoyed by my transformation. It wasn't going to save her, unfortunately, but it definitely made her happy, and if Nan was happy, so was I.

In hindsight, the only thing I regret missing out on from that period are some aspects of a more conventional social life for a man of my age: weekends away with the lads and stag dos. Apart from the very occasional night out, which would have been once every six months, I never once allowed myself to become distracted. At the end of the day if I had gone out on the piss more I'd only have got into trouble, and as a fine upstanding member of the community (ahem), I couldn't afford to do that. I was quite the little businessman really and it was only matter of time before I moved into even bigger and better things.

CHAPTER 13

Body Beautiful

Apart from my Mohican, my beard, my size, my sheer unbelievable brilliance and of course my modesty, I'm probably best known – visually, at least – for my tattoos. Though the effect that my very first tattoo had on my long-suffering mother, had I known it beforehand, would have made me think twice about having it done.

Whenever I'd spoken to my dad about tattoos he'd always echoed what his dad, my orange-slicing grandad, had told him: 'While you're living under my roof there'll be no drugs, no police and no tattoos.' I don't think he was really bothered either way but he repeated it just the same.

Rightly or wrongly (although it's usually wrongly with me), I'd already contravened two-thirds of that regulation and so it seemed a pity not to go for the hat-trick.

It all started off with a little bit of self-imposed peer pressure. As well as being a doorman and a truck mechanic, I was also an eighteen-stone body builder and without wanting to appear like a complete conformist, I seemed to be the only person in all three of these environments who didn't have any tattoos.

That's about as far as the conformity went though and so instead of following the crowd and getting a tattoo of a bulldog or whatever, I went the whole hog and got a Celtic tribal band that went from my elbow, up my arm, over my back, and then down to the other elbow. It took about forty hours in all and although it smarted a bit at times I was as happy as a pig in shit with the result and in my opinion it looks fantastic. That's me all over though. If I was going to get a tattoo done like everyone else, I could never get a tattoo like everyone else's, if you see what I mean. It had to be something different and it had to be something noticeable, otherwise, what's the point? These days people seem to enjoy having the same tattoos and haircuts and the big craze at the moment is having a short back-and-sides and a tattoo sleeve on your left arm. My gym's absolutely full of them. I know exactly how good it can feel fitting in, but when it comes to things like cutting my hair and putting a load of permanent ink on my skin, I prefer to be a forerunner as opposed to a follower. You lads carry on, though. Don't mind me.

It's something I actually thought about long and hard and the more I thought about it the more determined I became that whatever tattoos I got should match my personality. They had to be big, and they had to be bold.

Unfortunately, my poor mum wasn't quite as pleased with my body art as I was and the first time she saw it she burst into tears. Just for a split-second I thought it might be because she liked it, but when she cried 'Oh my God, Eddie, what the bloody hell have you done?' I knew that perhaps she wasn't exactly enamoured by it and I was left feeling a tiny bit crest-fallen. I still catch her scowling at my tattoos sometimes, but in all honesty, I think she's grown to like them. She'd never, ever admit it though. Dad, on the other hand, has gone one better and has had one done himself. If this paragraph makes it into the final book, incidentally, I'll be amazed – because, unlike his youngest son, Dad hasn't told his mum yet. Go easy on him, Grandma. He's a good lad really.

If I had a tenner for every time I've been called a paradox over the years I'd be able to put down a deposit on a house, and that's exactly what I did after having my first tattoo. Most people would go to the pub; I bought a house.

I had about ten grand in the bank at the time, which was about enough for a deposit, and apart from wanting my independence I knew for a fact that your average eighteen-year-old would never be able to afford to buy their own place and that made me feel like I was achieving something. I can find competition in pretty much anything!

The house I ended up buying is the house I live in today and it cost me the grand total of £115,000. That might not be very much by today's standards but it felt like an absolute fortune at the time and my God did I feel grown up. I remember thinking to myself, *I've just spent over a hundred grand. What the fuck!*

Less than a year later I ended up buying a second house, which is just a hundred yards up the road, but this was purely an investment decision. The idea came from a bloke I worked with at LEX Cobridge, who, without wanting to sound rude, was a bit of a wise fool. He was one of those people who seemed to know something about everything, without being a bullshitter, but despite offering lots of good advice and he rarely practised what he preached and so never benefited himself. I just don't think he had either the guts or the drive to follow any of it through, which is shame.

Anyway, he started going on about pensions one day and said, 'Why would you put 5 per cent of your wages into a pension scheme for thirty years, just so they can give you £200 a week when you retire? Buying a house is a much better idea.' This seemed to make perfect sense to me because as well as a house paying for itself via the rent it generates, and so not really costing you anything, you'd be able to cash it in whenever you liked. Being tied in to something like a pension scheme filled me with the same dread as being tied into a job for the rest of my life. It wasn't for me.

Anyway, before you start thinking I'm too sensible I should tell you about how I got another rather noticeable feature of my appearance. As well as my tattoos, the other thing people ask me about most with regards to my stunning good looks is the scar that runs over my left eye. Because it runs directly over the middle of my eye, and because it is very noticeable, some people think it's either make-up, which is bollocks, or that it was done deliberately, which is just beyond bollocks. I mean, come on. Regardless of how hard it might make you look, who in their right mind would get somebody to knife them across the eye?

In actual fact the scar was attained during an altercation that took place on Valentine's Day around the same time as I got my first tattoo, and, as with so many things, it isn't something I'm particularly proud of. I was out with a few mates of mine at a nightclub in Hanley and as well as being three sheets to the wind I was also wearing one of those Superman T-shirts (one of these days Superman's going to get caught wearing an Eddie Hall T-shirt!). Anyway, at about one o'clock in the morning this prat walked up to me and said: 'Oi, Superman. Reckon you're hard?'

Being me I replied, 'Actually, dickhead, yes, I do.'

'You want to prove it?' he said.

'Why not? Wherever you like.'

I then followed this knobhead out of the nightclub and as he walked his mates started joining him. *Here we go,* I thought. *Another fanny who can't fight his own battles.*

By the time we got out of the nightclub there were about twelve of these idiots and by the time we reached the road they all seemed to be carrying hand tools. Things like hammers and stuff. At first I thought they might all have been carpenters, but I was wrong. They were just tools.

The fight only lasted five or ten minutes but during the commotion one of them attacked me with a Stanley knife and that was the result. I only noticed it the next day and instead of going to the doctors I just left it to heal up. I was more concerned with my hands and my forehead. They were in a right fucking state! My knuckles were pitch black from where I'd been smacking these twats and the front of my head was covered in lumps from where I'd been headbutting them. I looked like a frigging Dalek! The eye was almost secondary really and became more noticeable once it had healed up. Before that it was just a wound so could have been an accident. People are fascinated by scars. Especially when you look like me.

These days I'm obviously a reformed character but I still get the odd prat asking to take me out occasionally. The only difference these days is that they're all on social media so they're probably hundreds or even thousands of miles away. Proper tough guys! I get things like 'I could do you with one punch, mate,' or 'You wouldn't last two minutes with me.' After having a laugh I just block them. There's no use getting involved. Best leave them in fantasy land.

While we're here I may as well go through the rest of my scar collection.

The other one people ask me about is at the top of my right cheek and it was a present from my brother James, bless him. We'd been having a scrap one day (after I'd been winding him up) and because there weren't any samurai swords knocking about the place he threw a piece of ice at me instead. Some of the things we used to do to each other you wouldn't do to your worst enemy. We've actually beaten each other unconscious before. As kids! It's crazy.

The next one's just above my lip but because of my beard you can't really see it. That was a result of being hit with a knuckle duster by one of James's friends and it actually made a hole in my face. This idiot used to get on my nerves and one day I got so fed up with him that I called him outside. We got split up after a couple of minutes but as I was walking away he shouted, 'Hey, Eddie,' and when I turned around he hit me just below my nose. You could see my teeth through the hole. It was gross! I didn't go down though and before I went to A&E I managed to get the boot into him a couple of times.

Last but not least is the scar on my eyebrow. That happened while I was snowboarding with some mates one day (in Stoke by the way, not the Alps). As we were trundling through the snow we came across a group of lads. Naturally, I couldn't resist mouthing off to them but before I could get an answer one of them hit me with a spade. My eyebrow looked like a fucking sausage and it took me a good few minutes to get my bearings.

Served me right really.

CHAPTER 14

Beginnings and Endings

The autumn of 2007 is a pivotal time in my life for two very different reasons. First, on 2 September, I entered my first strongman competition, which, bearing in mind what I do for a living, is pretty damn pivotal.

It was actually my brother James who first suggested I enter it and it was in reaction to my size. In fact, I think his exact words were: 'You've got to do something with all that fucking muscle, Ed!' I was lifting some ridiculous weights by this point and so I agreed. It was just for shits and giggles really but because there was competition involved that made it interesting. The advert for the event read as follows:

NOVICE STRONGMAN EVENT

2 September 2007

The Fitness Factory, Unit 5, Burnham Business Centre, Blannel Street, Burnley, BB11 4AJ

Athlete Registration 11 a.m. Start time 12 p.m.
Entrance fee – £10 to include competition T-shirt
Top three athletes receive competition trophy, next four competition medal
1st prize – £75 voucher *
2nd prize – £50 voucher *
3rd prize – £25 voucher *
* vouchers redeemable in Muscle Mass Supplements shop
CLOSING DATE FOR ENTRY 24TH AUGUST 2007
HEAD REFEREE – FORMER BSM MICK GOSLING
GUEST APPEARANCE AND TROPHIES PRESENTED BY MARK FELIX
THE EVENTS
1. Truck Pull: 7.5-tonne (16,500 lb) truck pull. 20 metres course. Time limit 75 seconds.
2. The Log Lift: 90kg (198 lb) for reps in 75 seconds.
3. Farmer's Walk: 90kg in each hand. 40 metres with turn. 75-second time limit.40-MINUTE BREAK
4. Deadlift: 190kg (418 lb) for reps. Time limit 75 seconds.
5. Tyre Flip: 350kg (771 lb) tyre to be flipped 8 times. 90-second time limit.
6. The Medley: 60kg (132 lb) barrel carried 20 metres, 90kg farmer's walk carried 20 metres, 100kg (220 lb) chain drag 20 metres.
This will be a very good show for first timers. Well organised with prizes. Come on guys, give it go.

I turned up to the event with no agenda and no idea what I was doing. Was I a fan of strongman then? Yes, I suppose I was really. I knew who the main protagonists were, people like Terry Hollands and Mariusz Pudzianowski. If you lifted weights they were the blokes you looked up to and when I found out Mark Felix was giving out the prizes I remember being quite excited. I'd met plenty of famous footballers before through door work but because I couldn't give a shit about the sport that never impressed me. They were just a bunch of rich idiots in my eyes. Mark Felix, though? He was one of the best deadlifters on the planet at the time and that did impress me. He was somebody I admired and wanted to meet. Terry Hollands was also doing really well then and because of his success there was a bit of a buzz around the sport. I was only there for a laugh though, and didn't know a tyre flip from a farmer's walk. Seriously! I had to ask for advice on almost every event. Where do I hold it? Where do I stand? What do I do? Apart from the standard deadlift I was new to it all and I remember people laughed at me for wearing weight-lifting gloves. I asked the referee once or twice if I was allowed and honestly, it was as if I'd farted the national anthem! I also remember doing the truck pull wearing standard Caterpillar boots, which was novel. None of the gear, no idea! It all took place in a car park somewhere in Burnley and there were probably about a hundred people there.

I can't remember the details of how I performed in each event but I definitely ended up finishing fifth out of fifteen.

This was OK bearing in mind I was so inexperienced and getting to meet Mark Felix was the icing on the cake. One thing I do remember from that day is noticing the difference in build between me and the other competitors. Although I was quite a big lad I was also very defined, whereas the others were a lot bigger and bulkier. Vanity was still part of my motivation then, but if somebody with the wrong build and no experience could come fifth in a competition, what would happen if they sacrificed their vanity for bulk and then gave it another go? I'd definitely got the taste for it.

Before I had a chance to do anything about it, though, something happened that was to break my heart and put all my other thoughts into perspective. The second reason why autumn 2007 is so pivotal took place on Monday 22 October and it is still the bitterest pill I have ever had to swallow. It was the death of my nan, who had been living with leukaemia for the last five years. I touched earlier on the closeness of our relationship but since her diagnosis that had deepened and she was so much more than just a grandparent. She was my friend, my confidante, my carer, and even my unofficial parole officer! I know it's quite an overused expression these days but more than anything, Nan was my rock. It must have been hard not to judge somebody as difficult and screwed up as me, but she never did. Not once.

My depression and anxiety had started soon after Nan was diagnosed which demonstrates just how much she meant to me. At the time, losing her would have been the worst thing that could have happened in my life and over the past five years I'd had to learn to live with the fear of that happening, just as Nan had learned to live with her leukaemia. The prognosis, and the condition, was obviously very different for me. I was young and strong and underneath all that crap going on inside my head was somebody normal-ish waiting to get out. And he would get out, eventually. For poor Nan, the condition and the prognosis were far bleaker and how the hell she held on for as long as she did amazes me. My God, I'm grateful for it. Leukaemia's one of those diseases that can kill you in a day, if it can, but Nan wasn't having any of it. She was made of sterner stuff and I'll always be enormously proud of her bravery.

This is the first time I have ever recounted the full story of my nan's passing and to be honest I've been dreading it. But it's got to be done.

It happened on a Monday, and because I'd been working the doors all weekend I'd decided to take the day off work. I remember feeling absolutely fucking knackered and in addition to this I'd had a big row with my girlfriend Laura the day before and was feeling very down and alone. Then, later in the morning, I received a telephone call from the hospital saying that my nan had been admitted, she was alone, and would I like to come up immediately.

My initial reaction to her admission was anger, because she'd expressly asked to die at home and the fact that this might be denied her infuriated me. Unfortunately, my grandad had very severe dementia at the time and, after finding her unconscious on the couch, he instinctively called an ambulance. Grandad had then started to panic and so while a neighbour looked after him, the paramedics took Nan to hospital.

When I got there I saw my nan very briefly before being asked to wait in a room. She was surrounded by people and when a doctor came to speak to me I was told that she was very, very weak and would probably die. He then asked me if I'd like them to resuscitate her and I said that we should respect her wishes and let her die with at least some dignity. That was so, so difficult for me because all I wanted Nan to do was live, but this wasn't about me, was it? This was about her and if she wasn't able to die at home like she wished, it was up to me, with the doctor's help of course, to ensure that she died as peacefully and painlessly as possible.

Straight after speaking to the doctor I went into Nan's room, sat by her side, held her hand and told her how much I loved her. Together with my parents, she had always been my most voracious supporter and whatever mistakes I'd made in life, Nan always believed I'd come good. Emotionally, she had underwritten every dream I'd ever had and so before she passed away I decided that we would share one more.

'Do you know what, Nan,' I whispered to her. 'One day I'm going to become the strongest man on Earth and when I do, you're going to be the proudest nan there's ever been.'

About a minute later, Nan slipped away and about five minutes after that the doctor pronounced her dead. The fact that I was there for Nan when she passed still means the absolute world to me and if she'd died all alone I don't think I'd ever have been able to forgive myself. I'm convinced she hung on, so I could be with her in her final moments.

For the next half an hour or so I just sat on Nan's bed, hugging her. Then, one of the nurses reminded me that perhaps I should make a few telephone calls and let people know, which I did. After that they moved Nan into a room where I could be alone with her and again I just sat there hugging her and asking her to come back. Many of you reading this will know what I mean but the realisation that you'll never see somebody again and the desperation that accompanies that is extraordinary and for a time I just couldn't get my head around it. We're not programmed to understand things like eternity and every time I remembered that I would never, ever see my nan again I'd experience a moment of blind panic, followed by a pang of overwhelming sadness.

My poor mum was having a final interview to become a fire fighter that day and Nan must have died while she was about halfway through the questioning. With Mum's phone being turned off I obviously couldn't get hold of her and so left messages instead. Once she eventually got back to me I told her what had happened and she was absolutely beside herself. I tried to reassure Mum that it had all been very peaceful but like me she was disappointed that Nan hadn't been able to die at home. It certainly wasn't anybody's fault but she'd been so adamant and I think we felt like we'd let her down a bit.

Almost as soon as Nan had passed I could feel what was left of my depression and anxiety lift, and, in a way, I'd almost been expecting it to. Had Nan known what I'd been going through and why, she'd have been absolutely devastated, but love can manifest itself in odd ways sometimes and while she was alive it was my way of expressing my grief at her illness. Why I couldn't have shed the odd tear like everyone else I'm not sure, but then, I don't do things by halves, do I? If I'm going to get upset when one of my favourite people gets leukaemia I'm going to do it properly!

Now she'd passed away, the depression and anxiety had been replaced by feelings of extreme sadness which meant I could mourn my nan, get on with my life, and, most importantly of all, remember all the fantastic times we'd had together. That's exactly what Nan would have wanted.

A much-needed highpoint after losing my nan was a request by my old swimming teacher, Greg Clarke, to come out of retirement and help out COSSACS in a medley race at a swimming competition in Wolverhampton. Greg said, 'Come on, mate. Let's have a laugh and see what you can do. See if the magic's still there.' Greg knew exactly how competitive I was and even though I hadn't swum for a couple for years I thought, *Why the hell not?* I'd get to see some old friends and regardless what had happened with Bill Sweetenham and, more regrettably, Arnold, I'd enjoyed my swimming days massively and I could certainly use a bit of enjoyment again after Nan's passing.

When it came to the race I even surprised myself and managed the 50-metre freestyle in just 25.8 seconds. Bearing in mind the current world record is 20.91 seconds that's pretty fucking amazing, especially when you consider my size. Being about twenty stone meant I was twice as big as every other swimmer there and so all things considered perhaps I should have considered returning to the sport. No flaming chance! The sport would have closed down if it thought I was returning. It was nice to dip my toes back in, though. I still get interviewed about swimming, by the way, and just recently I had about four or five pages in the *Swimming Times*.

By the time I was twenty years of age then I had a good job, my own business, two houses, a BMW Z3, a growing collection of amazing tattoos and a fifth place trophy won at a novice strongman competition in darkest Burnley. Who could ask for more? My apprenticeship had come to an end at LEX Cobridge but I still felt like an apprentice there, so I managed to get a job looking after a fleet of trucks at Robert Wiseman Dairies. As well as a certain amount of autonomy, the new job meant that my wages virtually doubled overnight. The trucks were also a lot cleaner and we had a great team spirit.

Everything was going well but even with all these distractions I thought a lot about Nan's passing. It was a watershed moment in my life and one that I will never forget. But life has a way of grabbing you by the balls sometimes and reminding you – rather forcibly – that with every end there is a beginning. And exactly one year after Nan died, I was to have a new beginning of my own.

CHAPTER 15

Baby on Board

On 28 October 2008, a year to the day after my nan passed, something happened that was to change my life forever. My daughter Layla, whose birth was obviously expected but certainly hadn't been planned, was born weighing six pounds and seven ounces, and with her came a brand new me. I remember I was obsessed with who was the hardest lad at high school. In fact, in the whole of bloody Stoke! That's not a healthy ambition for Christ's sake, and look where it got me. All of a sudden, the only thing that mattered in the world was Layla and it won't surprise you to know that I took fatherhood very, very seriously. Out went the sporty BMW Z3, and in came a family-friendly BMW X5. I even started working harder, which was barely possible, and I became totally focused. I suddenly had a reason for working hard and working out, apart from just bettering myself, and I had a goal, which was to be a good dad and to make Layla proud.

For the first time ever I began taking pride in myself, which is something I'd always found difficult. I'd sometimes taken pride in what I'd achieved, such as winning golds at the Nationals and deadlifting 260kg (573 lb), but that's a different thing altogether. One is all about you, and the other is all about what you can do. In order to take pride in yourself you first have to accept who you are, and with the depression now gone that was much, much easier to do. Nobody's perfect, but all in all I wasn't a bad lad and if taking pride in yourself means trying to be a better person, which I believe it does, I was going to give it my best shot; not just for the sake of my new-born daughter, but for the sake of me and for everyone around me.

Layla's mum, by the way, Laura, who I'm no longer with, had been my girlfriend since high school and we'd stayed together until I was about eighteen. Then, when I'd just turned twenty, we got back together again for a short time and the result of that reunion was Layla. I was able to be there for the birth, although I only came in right at the end, and it completely knocked me for six. It doesn't matter what you think you've achieved in life or how much money you've earned; watching a new life come into the world, one that you've helped to produce, moves you on to a much higher plane in my opinion.

As a result of me trying to take pride in myself I went from being somebody who was generally feared in the town and whose presence spelt trouble, to somebody who was respected and who was seen as being a bit of a gentle giant. Don't worry, I hadn't suddenly turned into Cliff Richard, and there was definitely no epiphany going on. I simply resolved to *try* to set a good example to my daughter and make her proud of me.

Nine years on and I still live by exactly the same rule, the only difference being that I now have two kids and a wife, so that's three times the motivation. That's how I look at it, anyway. When people who want to talk to me about strongman ask me what my goal in life is, I always say, 'To win the World's Strongest Man.' That's what they expect me to say and from a professional point of view it's correct. What I don't tell them is that by winning the World's Strongest Man I'll help maintain my ultimate goal of making my family proud of me. But what then? Having pride in yourself and being a good person is something you have to work at over an entire lifetime and so once that's out of the way I'll be onto something else. There's no destination, just a journey. And hopefully, a long one.

For all my talk of setting examples, I was still only twenty years of age when Layla arrived and when it came to my relationship with Laura it was one area where I'm afraid I failed to live up to my own hype. I used to receive a hell of lot of attention from women while I was working the doors and to be honest with you the temptation became too much. Laura and I had also been together for a long time, on and off, and it was the first and only relationship either of us had ever had. I think I was bored really. Not with Laura, but with the relationship. I know some of you will think I'm a bit of a hypocrite after what I said about setting examples, but I did say that I was no angel.

Layla's going to be nine this year and although she doesn't live with us she's only a minute up the road and we've got a very, very good relationship. I'm her hero, which I have to admit makes my sixty-eight-inch chest swell with pride. It hasn't always been easy and until I turned professional as a strongman my relationship with Layla had become a casualty of my all-or-nothing nature; the all being strongman, and the nothing being my relationships. Making people you love proud of you is all good and well, but when your efforts start to destroy those relationships something has to give.

Nevertheless, becoming a strongman became a huge focus for me at this time and, rightly or wrongly, I threw myself into it 100 per cent in my usual fashion. If I was going to be a strongman and make my new daughter proud of me, I was going to be the best fucking strongman she'd ever seen.

CHAPTER 16

Going National

Since entering the novice competition in Burnley I'd been like a man possessed and as well as upping my training a lot I'd started eating for England. There was no science behind it at the time. I just upped absolutely everything! I still wasn't expressly training for strongman at this point, by the way. That would come much later. I was just going through the usual muscle groups. In fact, the only specific training I'd done so far was when I attended a strongman camp at a gym in Stoke. I honestly couldn't tell you why this was the case and it's madness when you think about it. I just don't think it occurred to me. I'd just turn up to a competition, compete in all the strongman events, and then go back to just lifting weights in the gym. Talk about missing a trick!

With regards to how dedicated I felt, it was a carbon copy of what had happened with the swimming, except there was no Arnold Faulkner or Greg Clarke to help me. This was actually a positive, in the sense that I had nobody to fall out with, but not having any advice or experience to hand obviously wasn't ideal and the result of that was I was actually training to be a bodybuilder and not a strongman. This slowly evolved and although I carried on training as a bodybuilder I also started training all the strongman events. This meant that if I was training legs, for instance, I'd also do a farmer's walk. Or, if I was training chest, I'd do a log press.

In hindsight, this wasn't as bad as it sounds because if there's one environment I thrive in it's 'me against the world', and that's exactly what it felt like. I might well have been at the bottom of the ladder but as opposed to worrying about what I didn't have, I got off my arse and started researching and asking for help. That's one of the things I love about strongman: you're completely self-contained, and apart from physios and the like, the only people you can really fall back on in the sport are your fellow strongmen. I have to admit I found this quite difficult early on because I can be wary of other people – especially the competition – but once you learn to relax a bit and you realise you're in the same boat it's fine. At the end of the day you're not asking them out on a fucking date or anything, you're just helping each other out, and because the sport's not exactly rolling in cash we rely on each other to a point and that's a good thing.

The first competition I entered after Burnley took place in Northwich in Cheshire and I think it was a qualifier for England's Strongest Man, although I could be wrong. The reason I remember it so well is because I was competing against Mark Felix and the events were as follows:

- Hand-over-hand Vehicle Pull – 2-tonne 4x4, 70-second time limit
- Vehicle Lift – on frame, as many lifts as possible in 70 seconds
- 85kg (187 lb) Steel Log Lift – as many overhead lifts as possible in 70 seconds, head to head
- 150kg (331 lb) Conan's Wheel (lift and walk in a circle) – as many revolutions as possible
- Barrel Load – barrel ranging from 70–100kg (154 – 220 lb), loaded onto the back of a pick-up truck, fastest time wins
- Digger Bucket Lift – 60-metre course, furthest distance in fastest time

As well as beating Mark on a couple of events, the steel log lift being one of them, I lost to him by just three points. This was a defining moment for me because Mark had been a regular contender at the World's Strongest Man finals for a number of years and so was part of the elite. Beating him, even in two events, made me sit back and think seriously about my future. I was just twenty-one years of age and I'd been pipped at the post by one of the strongest men in the world in just my second competition. What would happen if I really gave this my all? I thought to myself, *I've got a fucking shot here. I could get to the finals of World's Strongest Man.* It still didn't click to start training the events properly, though. Berk!

There you go, brothers and sisters. If you ever want somebody to blame for me being a strongman, look no further than

Mr Mark Felix. I get on well with all the lads, but Mark's a really, really nice guy. He's very quiet, so we don't have much in common in that respect. He's one of the best though.

In July 2009, I entered the inaugural Staffordshire's Strongest Man competition in the market town of Leek and finished third overall. This was yet another defining moment in a way because as well as out-performing the majority of my more experienced rivals it was local to where I lived. An awful lot of people turned up to cheer me on: friends from school and mates from both of my jobs and from the gym. This was a massive boost for me because it resulted in recognition and you know how important that is to me. The only thing that pissed me off about the competition was the fact that I failed to win – but I knew it was only a matter of time.

Funnily enough, I came across a report on the competition the other day that was published in the *Stoke Sentinel* and as it was my first mention as a strongman I thought I'd include it.

The winner of the first-ever Staffordshire Strongest Man contest is ... from the Black Country.

Wayne Russell took first prize after winning the inaugural competition during Saturday's Leek and District Show.

He overcame nine other competitors, including Crewe's Wayne Tunstall and Newcastle's Ed Hall, who finished second and third.

In a remarkable test of strength the strongmen had to:

Lift a 105-kilo log as many times as they could;

Try to complete a 20-metre course while carrying 120 kilos in each hand;

Lift the back of a 280-kilo van for as long as possible;

Flip a 400-kilo, 5ft 8in-high tyre;

Lift five stones of various weights onto platforms of differing heights in the quickest time.

After winning, 36-year-old Wayne Russell said: 'It was a good event. I was confident I would do well.'

Wayne Tunstall was disappointed not to win but has just come back from injury. The 28-year-old, who is the reigning London's Strongest Man, Derbyshire's Strongest Man and UK Strongest Man North of England, said: 'I'm disappointed not to win but I've only just come back from an injury, so I'm pleased with how I've done.'

Bouncer Ed Hall, aged 21, who lives in the Westlands, said: 'I think it will be a great event to have every year, and there's been quite a lot of interest from the public.'

Crewe plasterer Simon Daniels came ninth in his first-ever strongman contest. The 37-year-old said: 'It's been a good event, especially considering it's the first one. I'll train hard this year and come back again.'

Noting that this is shorter than the original version – assume that's deliberate but in case it wasn't...!

That's the first and last time I include a report on me coming third. Never again!

But did you notice the difference in age between me and most of the other competitors? They were all seasoned campaigners whereas I was just a pup. Nobody knew who the bloody hell I was when I came onto the scene and with my tattoos and my Mohican they probably thought I was a right tosspot. In fact, I remember the way some of them used to look at me and they definitely weren't wishing me well. In reality, I wanted them to think I was a no-hoper as it made proving them wrong all the more satisfying; it was probably the first time in strongman that I started actively playing mind games with my competitors.

The last competition I entered in 2009, which was the annual Strongman of the North competition, gave me my first taste of injury in the sport yet still yielded a highly respectable seventh position. At the time I remember being disgusted with myself for finishing seventh but that was simply down to frustration and inexperience. Injuries are part and parcel of what we do and you have to learn to accept them. More importantly, though, you have to learn to go easy on yourself both physically and mentally and the more you beat yourself up about an injury the more detrimental it will become. For the last fifteen months I'd literally been going from strength to strength and when my knee suddenly went halfway through the competition I thought it was the end of the world. These days, as frustrating as an injury can be, I always try to take something positive from it. This might just be an opportunity to rest up for a few days but I'm always on the lookout for some preventative strategies and if I can figure out how I can prevent that injury from that happening again, it could actually end up being a worthwhile experience.

At the end of my first full year in strongman I had two podiums to my name, a knee injury and a lowly seventh. But they were just the headlines and despite looking OK on paper they belied an even more positive scenario. I was twenty-one years of age and twenty-one stone and, as well as a steely determination and almost unlimited amounts of energy, I had enough natural talent to keep *The X Factor* going for a hundred fucking years. Sooner or later all this would start coming to the fore and I promised myself that this time next year the world of strongman would have a new star in the making. I might not be top of the game yet, but when I turned up to an event the other lads would know exactly who I was and what's more they'd take me seriously. That was my immediate ambition at the end of 2009 and only a nutcase would have bet against me.

The first few months of 2010 were relatively slow strongman-wise but the competitions I did enter all yielded firsts – or, if I was injured or having an off-day, the odd second. Even when I did come second, I'd just become even hungrier, so either way I was walking away with a win.

These were all either local or regional shows but what I really wanted a crack at was one of the nationals. That's the only way I could progress now, and I knew that success in the sport was a forgone conclusion. Not because I said it would be, but because I'd worked my fucking arse off doing one hour of cardio and four hours weight training every single day.

My opportunity finally came at the start of May and began with a telephone call from a mate of mine called Dave Meer. Dave, who's a fellow Staffordshire lad, was an experienced strongman and unfortunately he'd had to pull out of the England's Strongest Man competition through injury.

'I'm going to put your name forward as a replacement, if you're game,' said Dave. 'You'll have to qualify, of course.'

'A mere formality, Mr Meer,' I replied.

After thanking Dave very much I put the phone down and immediately began thinking about what was to come. England's Strongest Man (now defunct), whilst not being the most prestigious competition on the circuit, always had a cracking pedigree and past winners included the likes of Terry Hollands, Laurence Shahlaei, Eddy Ellwood and Jamie Reeves, who'd won World's Strongest Man back in 1989. What really excited me was that whoever won the competition would be promised safe passage through to the following year's UK's Strongest Man competition, and that's when things started getting interesting. This was the break I'd been waiting for and there was no way I was going to balls it up.

Sure enough, I pissed the regional qualifier and so with that safely out of the way it was all eyes on the final. This took place in Teesside on Sunday 12 September, almost three years to the day after making my debut in Burnley, and to me that was not only a good omen, but a perfect indicator of exactly how far I'd come in the sport.

The final took place at the Old Billingham Business Centre, Chapel Road in Billingham and the events were as follows:

1: 28-tonne (61,729 lb) truck pull over 25 metres
2: Log lift, 130kg (286 lb)
3: Flip, carry and drag
4: Axle deadlift
5: Loading

The competitors, while not being part of the elite, were still some of the best in the country and the difference in class to the kind of competitors I'd been used to was noticeable. These boys were massive and as well as there being several who were taller than me, there were one or two who were touching thirty stone. What a fucking eye-opener! It didn't make me feel intimidated, exactly, because I knew I had the measure of them. What it did do, though, was give me an extra gear and because of that extra gear I ended up winning the competition by half a point. Half a fucking point! At the end of the day I wouldn't have cared if it had been an eighth of a frigging point, just so long as I won.

Once again, I came away from that competition thinking, *If I can win a national at twenty-two, what will I be able to do when I'm twenty-three?* My progression had been quite organic so far, and I had to be careful not to rush things. I was still very young but with three years' experience already under my belt I was also no longer a novice. With my immediate ambitions now met, I had to start thinking about some new ones. Well, it would obviously be the UK's Strongest Man next, but then what? Maybe qualifying for the World's? Nah, that would be impossible. Wouldn't it?

CHAPTER 17

My Better Half

Despite all the momentum that was building around my strongman career at that time, there was something else that occurred in 2010 that was to have an even more lasting effect in my life. The most important thing to happen to me during this period, apart from meeting Mark Felix and spending a Sunday afternoon in Teesside, was meeting my wife, Alex.

Anybody who knows me, or who has seen my documentary, *Eddie: Strongman,* will have some idea of what this woman means to me and how important she is to my very existence, but I'd like to expand on that slightly and at the same time explain how she helps me day to day. Don't worry, there's no need to get your violins out, but at the risk of sounding like a cliché I believe it's true when they say that behind every great man there is, more often than not, a much greater woman. Mark my words, they don't come much greater than mine. Some of you still might be wondering what this has got to do with being a strongman and once you've finished this chapter I hope you'll realise that it had everything to do with it.

Being a strongman, as I've already intimated, can be a very solitary existence. Some of that's self-imposed, of course, and some of it isn't. But every time you emerge from that isolation – whether it be returning from a competition, recovering from an injury or just coming back from the gym – having somebody there who will always be 'pro-you' no matter what is as important as any amount of dedication or endeavour. In fact, to a certain extent you rely on that person to even exist; partly because they often inspire you to succeed – which Alex does, together with our kids – and partly because you can't be dedicated or enterprising without having a solid home life. For me, that's the platform from which I achieve greatness and Alex both creates and maintains that. I've often said to people, either in person or on social media, that they should never, ever underestimate me or what I can achieve, and the person who gives me the power to say that – and mean it – is my wife.

I first met Alex at the beginning of 2010. I was obviously still working the doors and as well as being a bachelor with his own house I also had a hot tub. In fact, I was probably the closest thing to a playboy Newcastle had ever seen and some weeks I'd hold hot tub parties in the garden. George Clooney in Saint-Tropez I was not, but after having a few in town, my mates and I would invite a load of girls back and we'd all have a bloody good time. Would I like to elaborate on that? Absolutely not. Suffice to say these parties could often go on for a very long time and more often than not I'd wake up to find mates asleep on the lawn and all kinds of everything in the bloody hot tub.

Then one night a mate of mine rang up and asked me what I was doing. 'There's a few of us getting pissed in the hot tub,' I said to him. 'Why not come over, and while you're there, bring a couple of girls with you? The more the merrier.'

Although these hot tub parties only lasted a few months (in total, not individually!), they represented the closest thing I'd ever had to a regular social life and looking back they were absolutely tremendous. Seriously, if you're a young lad who wants to know why you should work your arse off, there's your fucking answer! Get yourself a good job – or two, if you can manage it – then buy a house and invest in a hot tub. You won't regret it.

Anyway, when this mate of mine eventually arrived, he had two girls with him and one of these was Alex. Although she was local to the area I'd never met her before and although she knew who I was it was only by reputation. I've never asked Alex if that was a good or a bad thing and I don't think I want to know.

This may sound like a line but honestly, Alex was very different to any girl I'd ever met before and we hit it off immediately. Usually, and forgive me if this sounds conceited, which it does, but nine times out of ten it was the girls who came on to me and so historically I'd never had to put much effort in.

With Alex, it was a bit of an about-change and because I really fancied her I decided to turn on the charm. I'm not sure if she noticed but I definitely gave it my all. She's a big girl, about six foot tall, and that's one of the things that really attracted me to her. That, and her sparkling personality, of course! In all seriousness, she really did, and does, float my boat massively in that department and I remember being amazed at how caring she seemed. The initial attraction, though, for both of us, was our height and build and by the time she got out of Mr Lover's hot tub we'd arranged our first date.

Over the following weeks Alex and I went all over the place and it's fair to say we became inseparable. She must have thought all her Christmasses had come at once when I suggested we go jet skiing one day.

'Where to?' she asked, probably expecting me to say Majorca or somewhere.

'Colwyn Bay,' I replied.

I must say that Alex managed to hide her disappointment very well and she even managed to say, 'Ooh, that sounds nice.'

My dad had a jet ski at the time that he used at Colwyn Bay and before I started working my arse off for a living I used to use it quite a bit. We actually had a really good day up there and because it was a jet ski I thought would be in keeping with my playboy image. Hot tubs in Staffordshire and jet skis in North Wales. It was pretty serious stuff.

Within a year of meeting Alex I'd already decided that she was going to marry me. She didn't know it yet, but she was, and so all I had to do was tell her. Having never proposed to anybody before, and being an incurable romantic, I knew that it had to be something special – and, if I was going to stick to my 'all-or-nothing' rule, something truly spectacular. Getting on one knee in Paris was never going to be good enough for me so I had to start thinking.

I forget where the idea came to me exactly but it was pretty convoluted and involved an aeroplane, some very large signage, my dad, my mum, my future wife (I hoped), my future in-laws, one of her grandparents, and me. It had more elements to it than you could wave a stick at but providing my dad remembered how to fly the plane, and providing my mum had put the signage out and had reminded Alex's dad and nan to stand outside and wave at the right time, then nothing could go wrong. Oh yes, and Alex had to be looking in the right direction at exactly the right time – AND, she had to say yes. Piece of piss.

The idea was that my dad, who'd had his pilot's licence a few years, would take Alex and I out for a nice romantic flight together from an airfield about an hour away from where we lived, which, as the crow flies, was just a few minutes or so from Alex's parents' house. 'I'll tell you what,' I said to Alex. 'Why don't we fly over your parents' house?' to which she replied, 'Yeah, OK.'

While all this was going on my mum was on Alex's parents' lawn laying out a huge canopy that read:

ALEX
WILL YOU MARRY ME?
X

All we had to do now was get my dad to fly over the house, which would be easy, and then get Alex to look down at her parents' lawn, which wouldn't be so easy.

Because Alex had been really busy at work (she works for a recruitment company) she hadn't seen either her dad or her nan in ages and so as an extra touch I asked them if they'd mind standing on the lawn and waving when we flew past. I'd already asked her dad's permission to marry Alex, which he'd given me, and I was so glad that he agreed to be involved. He and Alex's nan did wave, bless them. And then they waved again. I don't know how many times I had to ask my dad to fly over Alex's parents' house but it must have been three or four. 'Oh, look down there, Alex,' I kept saying. 'Isn't that your parents' house?' She just wasn't interested.

When Alex eventually did look down and saw the proposal, and her dad and nan, she was in tears. So before she could say no, I slid the ring onto her finger, gave her a kiss and told her that I loved her. Funnily enough, she never did give me a formal 'yes' to the proposal but I'm pretty sure she'd have said something by now.

We got married about a year later and so within two years of first meeting me over a steamy hot tub in Newcastle, Alex had become my wife. By the time we tied the knot she was already about eight months pregnant with our son Max so there was very nearly an extra guest.

When it came to the stag do I decided to keep it quite low-key and although we all had plenty to drink we had a few days to recuperate before the big day. There's nothing worse than people turning up to their own wedding pissed. Isn't that right, Eddie Hall! Unfortunately, I made the almost fatal error of going out for 'just a few beers' the night before the wedding and ended up forgetting concepts like 'bed' and 'sleep' and went straight to the church still pissed. This, as you can imagine, went down like an atlas stone at a basketball game and neither Alex nor any of her family or friends – nor any of mine, come to think of it – were in the slightest bit impressed. God knows what I must have smelt like, but it can't have been very nice.

Because I don't drink very often I tend to go a bit mad sometimes and my tolerance level has actually increased since my whisky drinking days. Because I'm so big it takes about ten pints to even have an effect on me, and at least twenty to send me on my way, plus four or five shots. This isn't some macho brag, by the way. I weigh over thirty stone, remember, and consume about 80,000 calories a week. Getting me pissed is like trying to fill a bucket with a hole in it.

Because of my faux pas I hadn't even written my speech, if you can believe it. Being this disorganised was a completely new experience to me. Fancy leaving it till your wedding day to find out what it's like – what a tit! It went OK in the end but it was the first and last time I've blagged something so important. Funnily enough, the reception was held in a marquee on Alex's parents' lawn and I think returning to the scene of the crime helped to improve matters. We all ended up having a fantastic day, no thanks to me.

Alex has been by my side since I first won England's Strongest Man and her role, with regards to strongman, is multi-dimensional and it takes in every aspect of what I do: the training, the recovery, the diet. Alex makes all my meals, and there's a lot more to that than just shoving some ingredients into a pan. There's a real science to it and Alex has bossed that on my behalf. She still works, by the way, so it's time she has to make for herself. Actually, it's time she makes for me. But by far the most vital contribution Alex makes to my career is all the emotional support she gives me, and believe me, my emotions match my frame. They're not small! I can go from nought to sixty in about a second and a half and when I lose it, I fucking lose it. Before meeting Alex the only person who could tame me and talk sense into me was Nan, so the fact that somebody has replaced her makes me a very lucky man. It doesn't matter how bad the problem seems or how insurmountable the challenge, Alex helps me see through all the crap and helps me to focus again. It's fair to say that if I didn't have her fighting my corner I wouldn't be where I am today.

There are a great many sayings and mottos that have become lost in the land of clichés over the years, and sadly this renders them almost stale and meaningless. There is one saying in particular though that I would like to liberate from this verbal scrapheap because it sums up exactly how I feel about Alex and offers a true and accurate description of the effect she has had on my life. That saying is 'She is the best thing that has ever happened to me', and if nobody else wants it, I'm happy to keep it for her. For Alex.

CHAPTER 18

Introducing the Spartan

Right, enough of all that soppy bollocks. Let's get back to business. I think 2011 and 2012 is when I came of age as a strongman, both in terms of success and ability, but also in terms of character and personality. The more successful I became, the more bombastic I became, and by the time I arrived in Belfast to compete at UK's Strongest Man in August 2011, I'd established myself not only as one of the best strongmen in the UK, but also one of the most famous. Or should I say infamous? The fame was in fact completely premeditated, because although it was quite natural for me to beat my chest and play up to the audience and the cameras, it was also necessary in order to A) get me some recognition and separate me from the crowd, B) help promote the sport, and C) make me some damn money.

Let me start from the beginning.

When I came back from winning England's Strongest Man, my first national title, I was expecting, rather naively perhaps, to receive at least some recognition; either a 'well done' from my mates, a call from a journalist or maybe an offer of some sponsorship. Not a fucking peep. The final was on a Sunday, and when I went into work on the Monday nobody said a thing and there were certainly no journalists creeping around the garage, let alone potential sponsors. It didn't seem to matter to anybody.

Don't get me wrong, I wasn't expecting John Inverdale to be kissing my arse or for Nike and Coca-Cola to be waving contracts in my face, but I had it in my head that by winning a national title – one of only two, at the time – I'd at the very least have the local paper giving me a call. The silence was absolutely deafening and it put me on a massive downer; it's one that I still get to this day after a show, and for similar reasons.

On the Tuesday I called the local paper and asked to speak to the sport's editor. He obviously had no idea that I'd won England's Strongest Man, and why on earth would he? He took all the details and said he'd run something in a day or two. On the Thursday I bought a copy of the paper and there, on page 26, in the bottom right-hand corner, was a paragraph made up of three short sentences under the tiny headline: 'Local Man Wins Strongman Competition'. What really got my goat was that on the previous page there was a three-quarter-page report on a six-year-old winning a fucking badminton competition. Little Timmy beats a few locals and he gets three-quarters of a page. Eddie Hall wins England's Strongest Man – almost killing himself in the process – and gets three frigging sentences. What an absolute kick in the dick.

I had three choices at this point: I either jacked it in and went and did something else, carried on whinging, or did something about it – i.e. grabbed the sport by its fucking neck and shook it until people started noticing me. I knew that the sport of strongman was well loved in the UK, and I also knew that the one thing it was lacking, apart from money and regular TV exposure, were characters, and without those characters that was never, ever going to change.

When I started swimming all those years ago I very quickly realised that the person who gets noticed (by the crowd, at least) isn't the one who puts in the best time, it's the one who shouts and screams the loudest. They're the people the crowd want to see and they're the ones they remember. It obviously isn't as prevalent in swimming as it is in other sports because it's so time-driven, but whenever I used to get called onto the blocks at a swimming competition, everybody used to stop what they were doing and look at me – and the reason they did that wasn't just the enormous bulge in my trunks, it was because I was the one who stood out from the crowd and made a big fucking noise. The fact that I was also a damn good swimmer made sure they kept their eyes on me in the pool, but even if I'd been an also-ran, I'd still have been the one they recognised the next time around. Even back then I knew, deep down, that one day this would be the making of me and would help me to separate myself from everyone else, not just in terms of recognition, but also performance. And, because of the mental effect my persona has had on my competitors – i.e. getting into their heads – that's often been the case. Clever, isn't it? I'm just a fucking genius.

Something else that interested me at that time was WWF. Not the wrestling itself, necessarily, but its protagonists. Once again it was a case of 'who shouts loudest gets the most attention' and that's what fascinated me. The guys who'd created brands around themselves were not only the ones receiving the most attention and signing the most autographs, they were also the ones making the most cash – and the longer I spent in strongman the more anxious I became to try to emulate that. We're all absolutely enormous for Christ's sake, and because we lift heavy things for a living and say 'AAAAARGH' a lot, we're crying out to be characterised.

Believe it or not, the Beast, as I'm known now, is the second persona I've had in strongman. The first, which I got from the film *300*, was the Spartan, and it served me well for about three or four years. I already had the Mohican from my swimming days, and with the beard, which I'd grown as soon as I was able, and the tattoos, I definitely had the look of a Spartan about me. Watching the film sealed the deal.

When I first started calling myself the Spartan, which was about 2011, some of the more established strongmen began taking the piss out of me on social media. I was still the new boy back then and for a time I was a bit of a laughing stock. Not to the spectators, by the way. They lapped it up, which is why I became so popular, so quickly. Some of my colleagues, though, were less than impressed and comments such as 'What a dickhead' and 'This guy's making himself look like a fool' started appearing on a certain website beginning with the letter F.

Oh, how things change.

About a year ago I was having a conversation with some people within the strongman industry about why my persona had caught on and why I had so many followers on social media. I wasn't bragging about it or anything. We were just talking about it as being a success story within strongman. Suddenly, one of the people who'd slagged me off piped up and suggested that all strongmen should give themselves a brand and while they were at it they should all start kicking and screaming a bit more. Well, you could have knocked me down with a fucking feather. I'm afraid I just had to say something. 'Hang on,' I said. 'I've been doing this since 2011 and if memory serves me correctly you were one of the first people to call me a dickhead and claim that I was making a fool of myself.' After that silence prevailed, not surprisingly.

These days, a lot of the upcoming amateur strongmen are giving themselves stage names and building brands and I think that's fantastic. After all, imitation is the sincerest form of flattery and as the man who pioneered the idea within the sport of strongman, I take that as a massive compliment. Because we perform in arenas now, as opposed to car parks, giving yourself a stage name and trying to create a brand is almost a necessity, especially if we're going to turn strongman into the sporting equivalent of WWF, which I believe is possible. I don't think the established guys should bother, though. Especially ones who called me a dickhead.

At the end of the day, you need to remember that ultimately you're there to entertain the audience, so you need to put on a bit of a show. And you have to be adaptable. For instance, English audiences like a little bit of humility, whereas Scottish audiences don't. They just want you to beat your chest and say that you're going to annihilate the competition, whereas English audiences want you to talk about how much you respect your opponent. I'm fine with both, but the alpha male in me will always enjoy the former a lot more. Scottish audiences are also harder to make laugh than the English, so again, you have to adapt and alter what you say. That's not necessarily a good thing for me, though, as the harder I try the more I swear.

The issue of money, as with the alter ego, also came to light when I entered UK's Strongest Man in 2011. Bearing in mind this was a televised event and Britain's flagship competition at the time, what do you think the winner got? Fifty grand? No chance. OK, ten then? Try taking away eight from that. That's right, you got £2,000 for winning UK's Strongest Man in 2011, which at the time wasn't even a month's wages for me. The trouble was that everybody just accepted it and so even the strongmen who did manage to win the odd competition were barely breaking even, which meant the rest were obviously losing money. How is a sport – which, remember, is no stranger to success – supposed to be taken seriously when even its most successful protagonists haven't got a pot to piss in?

Once again, I could easily have said, *Fuck this for a game of soldiers, I'm going to do something else.* But what would be the point in that? I already had two good jobs and if I'd wanted to rest on my laurels and become Mr Average I'd have done it years ago. Something had to change though and instead of the TV companies just paying a few quid for the rights and not giving a dick about the sport, a new idea was needed. Something mutually beneficial where the first priority would be the advancement of strongman and where the strongmen themselves would be remunerated, incentivised and made to feel involved. I wanted to be a partner in strongman, not a fucking pawn.

But all that was in the future. In the meantime, I had a competition to win. When I arrived in Belfast to compete at UK's Strongest Man, my ambition as a strongman was actually to be the best in the British Isles. Whenever I decide to do something and then start telling people about that ambition, such as cleaning up at the Nationals or having a body like Arnold Schwarzenegger's, it's because I consider it to be attainable. There's no point going public about a pipe dream, because the chances are you'll make yourself look like a twat. The reason I hadn't even thought about becoming World's Strongest Man

With my beautiful mum, Helen, on the day I was born – 15 January 1988.

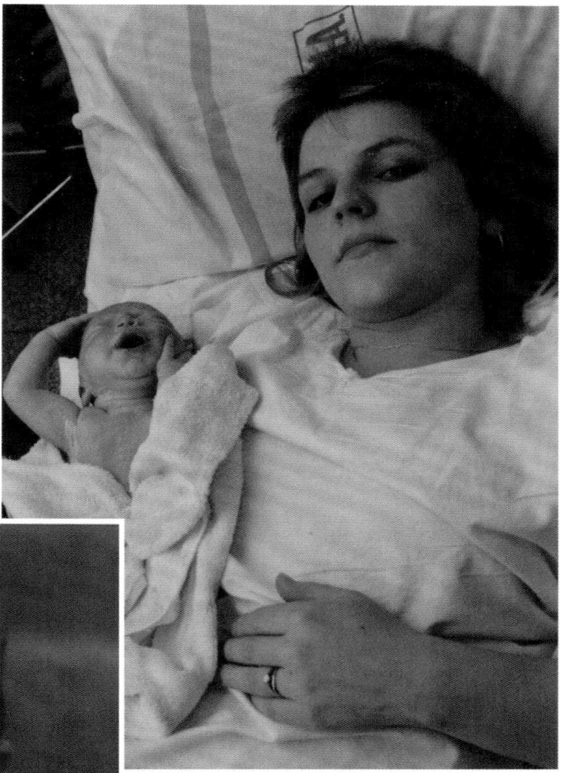

Me at five months old. Mum always said I was a happy baby.

My first bike. I was a pro rider straight off. The bike was a hand-me-down – always a problem of being a younger brother.

Me at nursery.

My brothers and me on Dad's pride and joy. One brother, unnamed, took it for a ride at 15 and binned it. You can guess what followed!

My first means of transport at 16.

On holiday in Portugal, 1993. We were always dressed the same on holidays and I will cherish these memories forever.

Aged 10 on my first day at a new school – the last school had had enough of me!

My brothers and me swimming on holiday in Portugal.

1995: I broke my arm falling out of a tree the day before we flew out on a holiday to Portugal. Nothing stopped me swimming.

1995: We were always trying to prove who was strongest, my brothers and I.

National Swimming Championships 2001: Arnold knew I was good but I don't think he expected four golds and a silver medal. Following this success, I was enrolled onto the World Class Potential Programme.

My first real feature in the local paper. I felt like a celeb.

Future star: Ed Hall. Photo: PAUL PICKARD.

NEWCASTLE star Ed Hall has been identified as one of the country's brightest prospects.

The 13-year-old has been selected for the world class potential programme organised by British Swimming and will attend training weekends at Leeds international pool during the next four months.

Hall will be joined at the camps by Newcastle swimming coach Arnold Faulkner who will help train the youngsters.

Hall's selection follows his phenomenal success at the national championships this year where he claimed four titles and set a new British record.

Here I am, aged 14 and weighing 14 stone. This was taken after completing Swimathon, a 5km charity swim in support of cancer. I completed the course in 1:01:15.

I was 16 and 16 stone when this picture of me was taken. I am taking part in my last National Swimming Championship in Sheffield, 2004.

2002: Me, Nan and Grandad Jackson after winning four golds at the Nationals. This was a proud moment for all the family.

Our family jet ski was responsible for many great memories, including (nearly) getting lost at sea.

My first car, a BMW 316. I was 17 and the coolest kid on the block.

At 14, I started lifting weights during my training to help keep me out of trouble.

My brothers and me after our charity swimathon. We would always do our bit for charity and we're holding our certificate of recognition here.

July 2003: 15 and 15 stone.

Teen shows his strength

TEENAGE strongman Edward Hall finished in a respectable fifth place after battling through the rounds in his first contest.

The 19-year-old, of Eleanor Crescent, in the Westlands, went up against other musclemen at the event in Burnley.

In heavy rainfall, the truck mechanic gritted his teeth through events including the tyre flip, log lift and truck pull.

It was Edward's first big strongman event and he has now developed a taste for it.

He said: "I saw the advert and everyone kept encouraging me to take part.

"I will definitely do more, I'd eventually like to get to the World Strongest Man competition"

Also taking part was fellow competitor Mark Hill, of Bucknall, who finished in eighth position.

He added: "I was very pleased with that, as there were a fair few experienced competitors."

Burnley 2007: My first ever tyre flip in my first Strongman Competition, aged 19.

Burnley 2007: Mark Felix, the first World's Strongest Man competitor I met.

December 2010: The first competition where I began to show confidence and showboat – hence topless.

Family gathering on the occasion of my son's christening.

On a family holiday in Portugal. My brothers and I have had over twenty years of practice lining up for family pictures, as you can see from these.

June 2012: The day I married my queen. Alex was eight months pregnant with Max. I'm a very happy man here.

My first family photo shoot. I think the kids look so nice here.

Winning my first UK's Strongest Man competition. I set a record of 1m 18s whilst holding 20kg in each arm.

The 2014 Deadlift Championships at Europe's Strongest Man. This is the moment I dropped the World Record Deadlift… bad times!

Redemption. World Record 462kg at the Arnold Classic, Melbourne 2015.

Photo shoot for a new clothing line, Xplosive Ape. I am usually free for modelling jobs, by the way.

Chatting with my new pal Arnie... *I'll be back!*

Pulling an ancient double-decker bus at Europe's Strongest Man 2017. A very hard pull.

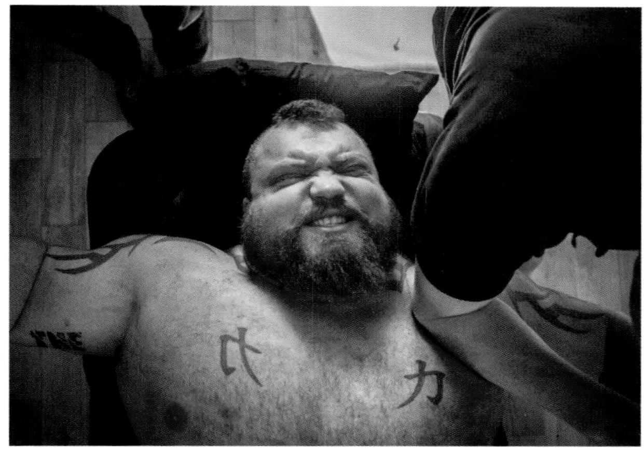

One of my many brutal physio sessions, it often brings tears to my eyes.

Me and Mo during one of our many catch-up meetings, running over business ventures and appearances.

Here's me in the hyperbaric chamber that I built myself. Alex, my wife, is taking the picture.

Sitting in 9°C water to aid recovery. My balls would disappear but it was all worth it!

Pushing the limits with a 500kg World-Record-breaking deadlift. To this day, this is the most dangerous thing I have ever done.

(although I had dreamed about qualifying for the competition), is because it was unknown territory and if I'm ever unsure about what, or who, I'm up against, I'm not going to start mouthing off. Some of you might find that hard to believe, but it's true. I'm confident and cocky, not daft and dopey. I might let my mouth run away with me sometimes but I rarely set myself up for a fall. I obviously knew what the field was, going into the competition, and I was confident of winning.

The competition was held over three days and the events were as follows:

Day 1

Duck walk and drag 40-foot lorry and trailer 20 metres x 1 competitor

Strongman flag hoist, five flags to be hoisted x 2 competitors

Human wheelbarrow, 20 metres, 90 seconds timed, 1 competitor

Arm wrestling x 2 competitors

Day 2

Deadlift car hold, straps, maximum x 2 competitors

Conan's torture circle, 360 degrees, 90 seconds x 1 competitor

Axe barbarian crucifix maximum hold x 2 competitors

Tyre flip, 20 metres, 90 seconds, 3 competitors

Final

Arm over arm anchor and chain, 20 metres, 90 seconds x 4 competitors

Axle for maximum x 1 competitor

Ultimate strongman shield carry, distance carried x 2 competitors

Squat for reps, 90 seconds x 1 competitor

Stones of strength, 100kg–160kg (220–353 lb)

I watched a recording of this competition the other day and my God did I stick out like a sore thumb. But in a good way. Most of the other competitors are big, bald and quite sedate, whereas I'm like a white B.A. Baracus on fucking acid. What an absolute gobshite! At the end of one of the arm-wrestling bouts, which I won beating a former Irish arm-wrestling champion, I let out this huge evil laugh and then screamed something that sounded like 'OOOOOJAAAAH!' My opponent was not impressed. A lad called Rob Drennan beat me in the final of that event and as he's getting the better of me I'm shouting and screaming like somebody's sawing my fucking leg off. That was how desperate I was to win.

They interviewed me at the start of the competition and who do I begin rabbiting on about? Arnold Schwarzenegger. 'What's your big ambition?' the presenter asked me, and I said, 'To be on television like Arnold Schwarzenegger.' When he looked at me like I was a cock, I shrugged my shoulders and said, 'Well, it could happen!' That was my first televised event, and it has to be said I looked like a natural.

During the truck pull, which I won, all you can hear is Alex shouting, 'COME ON, EDDIE!' She almost drowns out the bloody commentators. This, I'm afraid, became a bit of a bugbear of mine and over the years it started to get more and more annoying. It's not just Alex, by the way. In fact, my mum's the worst. She's only about five foot three inches, but she's got a voice like an amplified foghorn in the bottom of the Grand Canyon. Don't get me wrong, I absolutely love having my friends and family around me, but because I recognise their voices it can be distracting when I hear them during events. This came to a head at World's Strongest Man a couple of years ago when, half way through the truck pull, I started hearing this voice. 'Take little steps, Eddie!' it said. 'Take little steps!' It was Mum and the more I tuned into her voice the more annoyed I became.

Because the TV cameras were on me I obviously couldn't say anything but inside I was shouting, 'WILL YOU SHUT THE FUCK UP, MOTHER! I AM TAKING LITTLE FUCKING STEPS AND I'M TRYING TO PULL A MASSIVE FUCKING TRUCK!'

She obviously meant well, bless her, but after that I set a rule that friends and family had to remain silent during competitions, especially during a bloody truck pull. Little steps my arse!

I ended up winning UK's Strongest Man by half a point and went back home a reasonably happy man. It was televised later in the year and I got a real buzz out of telling all my mates I was going to be on TV. If I hadn't won though, I wouldn't have told a soul.

CHAPTER 19

Losing a Contest

In early 2012, I got meningitis. As you do. I was at work one day and as I was levering a bar down to test a suspension bush the bar slipped and smashed me in the nose. It was a bit of a mess but I carried on working. I'm dead hard, me!

Two days later I came down with a really bad headache at work. It was so bad, in fact, that I could hardly see anything and so I ended leaving about an hour early. Not that hard, then!

On the journey home, the lights from the oncoming traffic set the headache off again and when I got home I just collapsed on the sofa. Fortunately, my mum came over about half an hour later to drop something off and when she saw me on the sofa I was completely non-responsive. Couldn't speak, couldn't move, nothing.

Mum called an ambulance and after having a few tests at the hospital they confirmed that I had bacterial meningitis. Alex was pregnant with Max at the time and I was terrified I'd given it to her. Apparently, meningitis can lie dormant in your nose and if it gets disturbed it can become active quite quickly. Not everybody has it, but if you have and you have a nose injury you could be in trouble. I was off work for about two months in all and it really put me back.

This was the catalyst for making me give up the door work and as soon as I was back on my feet I sold the business. Despite the meningitis my immune system hadn't been firing on all cylinders so a near-death experience was exactly what I needed. It was a bit extreme though!

My first competition of 2012 took place in March and was a Giants Live event called the Melbourne Classic (now the Arnold Classic). Whoever finished inside the top three got immediate passage through to World's Strongest Man which was taking place that September. In the end I finished fourth, but a guy called Colin Bryce, who runs Giants Live with Darren Sadler, was so impressed by my performance that he took me to one side after the competition and told me that he'd make sure I won qualification. This was a colossal boost for me because I was confident that by the time September came around I'd have shortened the gap between me and the world's elite. With that being my only barometer it was imperative that I made it to Los Angeles, which is where the competition was being held.

Colin did have one issue, though. I was now starting to bulk up a lot and if I wasn't working or training, I was either eating or thinking about eating. Obviously, I needed to get bigger, but at the same time I had to try to maintain my fitness and mobility. Static power's important, but roughly half the events at World's Strongest Man require movement and if I wanted to challenge the athletes who were, perhaps, more genetically gifted than I was, I couldn't afford to have any weaknesses. When Colin told me that he intended to get me to Los Angeles he questioned whether my mobility was up to scratch and to be brutally honest, no, it probably wasn't. This is because I still wasn't training for strongman and so all I did from a training point of view was to lift weights.

Even so, I was still quite taken aback by Colin's comment and so parried it by informing him that I used to be a national swimming champion (which obviously requires a certain amount of mobility) and that I still held several records. I could tell by the look on his face that he thought this was bullshit and so I thought, Right then, Mr Bryce. Not only will I prove to you that I can move well with weights, but I will also prove that I was once the toast of the swimming world. Until I pulled that moonie and called Sweetenham a fat twat, of course.

Sure enough, when we finally got to LA I pulled out some of my press cuttings and very proudly handed them to Colin. He actually knows Mark Foster and when I'd told him that I'd broken one or two of Mark's records he once again thought I was pulling his plonker. I'll never forget the look on his face when he started reading the articles. While Colin's eyes started widening, a self-satisfied grin began permeating my face, which, if it could have been translated into words, would have said, 'What do you think about that then, eh?'

One of the reasons I was so keen for Colin to read those articles is because he was somebody I looked up to and admired. I may be a narcissist with a big gob but there are certain people in the world who make me want to shut up and listen, and Colin's one of them. It's the same with strongmen. I made a point, around this time, actually, of getting to know people like Brian, Thor and Big Z, for the simple reason that they were the best and I wanted to feed off their success. I also get on really well with them, which helps. Some strongmen would probably feel either intimidated or deflated by hanging around with people who are on a different level to them, but not me. If I was ever going to match, or perhaps even better, these inspirational behemoths, I had to know what made them tick, and, over the years, I've picked up all kinds of stuff – everything from eating habits, through to how they respond to certain situations and how they prepare for certain events. You can't always tell what they're thinking, of course, but being close to them means you often get a pretty good idea. Conversely, I think they've also picked things up from me. Especially since I've moved up to their level of size and strength. I've definitely taught them one or two new words!

When it comes to sport, Colin has been there, done that and bought the T-shirt; as well as being a former Olympic bobsledder he also spent time as a strongman and is one of the best sporting commentators there is. Ever since I first met Colin all he's wanted to do is help the athletes get on and he's advised me in every aspect of my life, from how to train to how I should conduct myself. Intellectually, he's a powerhouse but what I take away most from our relationship, apart from his friendship, is his wisdom. Colin has this knack of pulling things he's either heard or read out of thin air just at the right time and he's a constant source of inspiration.

A few years ago, Colin spent some time with Mike Tyson and when he asked him what Muhammad Ali had over everyone else he said that Muhammad Ali was the only one prepared to swim into dark waters.

'What do you mean, dark waters?' I asked Colin.

'Well,' he said, 'if all the greatest boxers swam out to sea, Muhammad Ali would be the one who'd keep swimming no matter what. He'd be the only one willing to swim into dark waters.'

That story of Colin's stuck with me big time and it describes my attitude to a T. To get where I want to be I am prepared to swim into the very darkest waters and regardless of what I do in life that will never change.

Funnily enough, that's not the only story that resonates with me that came out of this conversation between Colin and Mike Tyson. When the two of them got on to the subject of Ali calling himself the greatest, Tyson told Colin that Ali pinched that saying from a wrestler who was around in the 1940s called Gorgeous George. Being a good wrestler wasn't enough for Gorgeous George and so he invented a persona for himself that he knew would piss off his opponents. Back then, men were supposed to be men, so in order to have the most impact, George started turning up to fights wearing frilly bathrobes and platinum blonde wigs. He even used to enter the ring to Elgar's 'Pomp and Circumstance'. Not only would this infuriate the other wrestlers but it also gave George an immediate advantage. There was no way in the world his opponents could lose to a man dressed like that but because he was so effeminate they were afraid of going anywhere near him. It was absolute genius when you think about it and he turned the hitherto niche sport of wrestling into a huge hit. Apparently Muhammad Ali had seen George camping it up on TV one day, saying, 'I'm the greatest.' This obviously struck a chord with Ali and the rest, as they say, is history. That's where he got his big-talking public persona from and helped to make him a star.

When Colin told me this story everything just clicked into place and I could see how much of my own behaviour mirrored that of Gorgeous George's. I remembered how that public persona had come instinctively to me back when I was starting out as a swimmer – the bragging, the mind games, the flamboyant entrances … even the cross-dressing! Obviously like George and Muhammad Ali (or Cassius Clay, as he was then), I had to back up the showmanship with talent and ability, but the character also helped to give me the edge. Yet again, Colin had helped to give me an insight into my own personality.

When I found out I'd qualified for the 2012 World's Strongest Man I almost exploded. For a start it was going to be held in Los Angeles, which is somewhere I'd always wanted to go, and at the time, qualifying for the competition represented the sum of my ambitions within strongman. I'd make a judgement as to whether I'd alter this ambition after the competition had taken place, but in the meantime, I was just happy to be taking part.

I'll tell you something, though, it was a good job I had built my ambitions around what I knew, because when I got to the hotel and had a good look at the competition I felt like a little girl. I was twenty-four stone, for Christ's sake, but I genuinely felt minuscule. Every single athlete seemed to be huge and when I first saw people like Brian Shaw, Hafþór (Thor) Björnsson and Žydrūnas Savickas in the flesh, I almost packed up and started hitching a ride home. Not only were these blokes tall, especially Brian and Thor, but they were also as heavy as fuck and they were all about thirty stone. A six-stone difference might not sound like much to some people, but when you add to that a height difference of about six or seven inches, things start taking on a new light. Actually, those two mammoth freaks usually block out most of the light!

I suppose it was another Arnold Schwarzenegger moment in a way, but this time it was in triplicate, and, it was in the flesh. These three athletes have all taken the title of the World's Strongest Man and were so far and away better than everybody else it was ridiculous.

Despite feeling like a Jack Russell nipping at their heels I still thought I had it in me to get through my qualifying group and at least make it to the final, but unfortunately it wasn't to be. I did win a couple of events – the Viking press and the squat – which I was pleased with, but it was a difficult group to get out of and at the end of the day I was neither big enough nor good enough to progress, and finished the group in fourth place. Normally they use things like barrels for weights in the Viking press but this time they were using quad bikes and given my history I was always going to win that. It was a pyrrhic victory though and sometimes you have to hold your hands up and admit defeat. It's not something I find easy but once I get over the disappointment, the first thing I do is start looking for positives, and in this case, they weren't too difficult to find. I was still young and, although I wasn't big enough or good enough at the time, I had the makings of becoming a true behemoth, in every respect.

One thing I remember at the end of the competition was watching a photograph being taken with six different winners of the competition. There was Big Z, Brian Shaw, Bill Kazmaier, Magnús Ver Magnússon, Svend Karlsen and Phil Pfister.

I remember standing behind the cameraman thinking, *what an absolute fucking privilege*. Everybody – all the athletes and crew – were in awe of these guys and it was a great moment. Privilege aside, my one overriding emotion as I stood there watching them all was envy. Pure envy. What a motivation though.

Competitively, World's Strongest Man 2012 really opened up the world of strongman for me. In fact, it was like discovering a whole new continent. One populated by ugly-looking giants from America, Iceland and Lithuania, who ate, breathed and slept strongman; and who, unless I did something about it, would swallow me for breakfast every day of the fucking week. It was sink or swim time again. And, as per usual, I had three choices: give it all up and be happy mending trucks, consolidate my position as the strongest man in Britain, or start eating like a horse, training like a maniac and swinging from the chandeliers before finally mixing it with the big boys. It was time to start building the beast!

The rest of 2012 was a bit up and down really. I won UK's Strongest Man again, and won convincingly. Then I made my debut at Europe's Strongest Man at Headingley Stadium in Leeds, and it was like the Worlds all over again. I certainly didn't perform to my best but with Thor and Žydrūnas in the line-up it was a reminder not only of where I needed to be, but where I would be once I'd finished. I was now training specifically for strongman, at last, and that was already paying dividends. It had taken me a while but instead of just lifting weights I was training each specific event. The equipment didn't always match, but it was a step in the right direction.

CHAPTER 20
A Dramatic Arrival

Before we move on to 2013, there's one more event from 2012 that I have to tell you about, although it's nothing to do with strongman. This was a thousand times more stressful, although on the up-side I didn't have to lift a finger. The event in question was the birth of my son, Maximus, who was born on 10 July.

Maximus had been planned; Alex and I had even spoken about having kids on the day I asked her to marry me. We'd chatted about all aspects of our future that day and in celebration of our new life together Alex came off the pill the next day. About three months later she sat me down and told me she was pregnant, so as well as being a planned baby, he was a bloody quick one too. He ended up arriving four weeks after our wedding day.

Unlike I had with Layla, I actually managed to attend the birth from the start this time around. But the labour itself was very long and about half way through I actually went away to train for a few hours. That might sound a bit off to some people but hey, life goes on. That's my job and if I don't train,

I don't get paid. The midwife said I had plenty of time so while Alex was panting away in the hospital, I was pumping away in the gym.

A few hours later I was back in the hospital with Alex and because I was knackered after training I crashed on the floor and started nodding off. Suddenly, I heard an alarm going off and when I opened my eyes all I could see were red flashing lights and Alex being wheeled off by some nurses. I leapt to my feet to follow them, and fortunately one of the nurses waited behind for me to tell me what was happening in response to my frantic questions. Apparently there was a problem with Maximus's heartbeat and they were going to have to give Alex a caesarian. Poor Alex had lost consciousness by now and even though I was only peering in through a window in the door she seemed to be in a really bad way. These few minutes were some of the worst of my entire life and for all that time – which felt like eternity – I honestly thought I was losing them both. The feeling of helplessness was unbearable and when I eventually heard Maximus scream for the very first time, after being delivered by caesarean section, I almost collapsed with relief. It was like being pulled out of a fiery pit.

About five minutes later I was allowed into the delivery room and was able to hold Maximus for the first time. Alex was still unconscious at this point and although they'd told me several times that she was going to be OK I was still as nervous as hell. Not only do I love Alex to pieces but I need her, and now Maximus needed her. I'm not sure how I would have coped being a single parent but I wouldn't have fancied my chances much. I'm OK lifting weights on my own but bringing up children is much bigger task. Probably the biggest.

Fortunately, the doctors were right and a few minutes later Alex came around. She was still very poorly but she was alive, which was the main thing. Is it possible to measure extreme relief? Well, if anyone ever wants an example of somebody who is literally on their knees with it, then look no further than me on 10 July 2012.

The one thing people always want to know about Maximus is where we got his name from and because I'm tremendously proud of it I'm always only too happy to tell them. The first thing they usually always say is, 'Only you could call your son Maximus, Eddie!' and that's fucking bang on. Come on, it's the coolest name on the planet, right? I first got the idea when I watched the film *Gladiator* and that would have been in my mid-teens. I was obsessed by the film, just like I was obsessed by *The Terminator*, and when I first watched Russell Crowe introduce himself as Maximus Decimus Meridius, I remember thinking, *Fuck me, that is a proper fucking name!* It was pure power. At that moment I promised myself that if ever I had a son I would called him Maximus. I wasn't bothered about the other two names. They sounded like diseases.

Whatever Maximus ends up doing in life, and I know it's going to be something special, the moment he shakes a person's hand and says, 'Hi, I'm Maximus, how do you do,' they're going to think to themselves, *Wow, what a great name*. And, if he ends up being a big lad like his dad, which he probably will be, it'll make it even more impressive. I hope to God he doesn't end up being five foot five inches and about ten stone with a name like that!

When Alex was pregnant with Maximus we went and had a scan and when they told us what sex he was I was like a kid at Christmas. I'd kept on saying to the nurse who was doing the scan, 'It'd better be a boy. Seriously, it'd better be a fucking boy!' God only knows what she thought I was going to do if it hadn't been. I actually think I'd have just sulked for a bit. It's not that I have anything against girls, by the way. Layla's testament to that. Let's face it, though, there are only so many future boyfriends you can beat up, so us having a boy was better, and safer, for everyone concerned. Will I be a protective father? What do you think! Of course I will. I'll be fair though and I've promised Layla that she'll be allowed to date boys the moment she turns fifty.

The effect Maximus's birth had on me was very similar to Layla's in that it reminded me of my responsibilities and prevented me from acting like a prick. It wasn't as if I'd fallen off the wagon completely, but it was a timely reminder all the same, and because of this I became a lot more self-aware. By now I'd given up working the doors and so my only source of income was the day job. This was obviously a positive with regards to my family life but the effect it had on my bank balance was anything but. Despite Alex also bringing in a wage, the lack of decent income was starting to bother me. Food alone was now costing about £250 a week and that was just for me! I couldn't let it get to me. Only two things mattered now: succeeding in strongman and making my young family happy and proud. It was a self-fulfilling ambition, potentially.

However, there was a danger with this ambition that was always present too: that the very process of me attempting to become the strongest man on the planet wouldn't make my family being happy and proud, but it would have the opposite effect on them. It was something I was going to have to learn how to manage the hard way over the next few years.

CHAPTER 21

Planes, Trains and Automobiles

World's Strongest Man 2013 was an experience I will never, ever forget, and for all kinds of reasons. Good and bad. It started off with me almost murdering a Chinese teacher on a plane, and finished with me being the eleventh strongest man on Earth. But before we get into all that, let me tell you about something that, as I've become bigger, has caused me no end of bloody problems. Namely, travel. The bane of my life.

I think I first noticed it becoming a problem when I was about nineteen years old, and so nineteen stone. That was the point I realised that things like cars, trains and aeroplanes hadn't been designed for people like me. I seemed to have outgrown pretty much everything and the more I travelled, the more I noticed it, and the more I noticed it, the more it got on my frigging nerves.

Even short flights can be a nightmare and after only an hour on a plane I'll already be suffering from swollen feet, a bad back and swollen legs. Sometimes my feet actually double in size which makes it impossible for me to put my trainers on afterwards.

As I've become bigger so have the problems, and since I hit about twenty-four stone it's become almost impossible to get around easily, whether I'm travelling by train, plane or coach. When it comes to cars I have to buy American models and at the moment I'm driving a big Chrysler 300. Even that's become a struggle; in addition to having to lean away from the door pillars constantly it's murder on my back. They also cost a fortune to run, but then isn't that the rule? The bigger you get the more fuel you need.

This isn't just a rambling complaint, by the way. I'm just telling you what it's like. If I were that bothered I wouldn't have chosen to live my life this way, but this is what I do. You could stick me on ten-hour flight with no sleep, and I'd still get off and break a world record. In fact, I did once. I'll tell you about that in a bit.

The mode of transport that causes me the most amount of hassle, and the one I'll do literally anything to avoid (although that's difficult), is air travel. And, as I alluded to earlier, as well as almost being the death of me, both physically and mentally, it has pushed me to the brink of committing homicide – not just once, but on numerous occasions. That would make an interesting interview:

'So, Eddie. What would you like to do if you weren't a strongman?'

'I'd like to kill people on aeroplanes.'

Take April this year, for instance. I had to go to Frankfurt for an Expo and when I got to the gate at Manchester Airport I was denied access because of my size. 'You'll need to buy an extra seat, sir,' said the jobsworth in charge, 'Otherwise you will not be flying with us today.' Everything was too much trouble for this arsehole but instead of hammering him into the ground like I should have and then letting out an evil laugh, I just took a deep breath, shot him a look that said, 'Next time, wanker,' and then called the sponsor and asked them to buy me another ticket, which they did. I'll tell you what though, he was right. Even with two seats I only had about a centimetre either side of me and virtually no bollock space. Some of you might have seen this on my documentary but the acid test for me with regards to how I cope on a flight is how much bollock space I've got. If my balls can breathe, I can cope with just about anything. If they can't, somebody will probably die, and it won't be me.

Long-haul flights are obviously the nadir of my travelling life and before I board any plane for a long-haul flight there are two things I simply have to do: swallow a handful of diarrhoea tablets, and take a good long shit. Taking a dump on an aeroplane is almost a physical impossibility for me. In fact, the only way it might work is if I reversed in, but that's a big if. One thing I wouldn't be able to do is close the door and as somebody who eats around 12,000 calories a day you would not want to be within fifty yards of me when I'm on the throne.

Then, there's the small issue of cleaning up after myself, which I'd have to do in the aisle. Not a nice image, is it? I don't mind, but I have a strange feeling that the other passengers might just be reaching for the oxygen, if not the sick bags.

When I was on the flight to Frankfurt I had to go for a piss but because the toilet was so small I had to pee with the door ajar. One of the hostesses was horrified at this and started having a go at me.

'Sir!' she said. 'You can't do that. It's against the law.'

'What the hell do you expect me to do?' I said to her. 'I need a piss, for Christ's sake. If you want to try and close the door behind me, go ahead.'

This air hostess did try and it must have been hilarious watching her. She couldn't do it though.

To be fair, most people are quite good-humoured when it comes to this sort of thing and generally I rub along well with the airline staff. Occasionally though, you'll get a jobsworth and when that happens, sparks usually fly, and when sparks fly, I get into trouble. Whenever I'm going through security I always ask if I can go through the FastTrack lane because of the pain in my back and generally they give me the nod. 'Yes, of course, sir. Off you go. No one's looking.' When I'm in heavy training I can't stand for long and even after five minutes in a queue my back will be in agony. This before I've even got on the plane.

There was one little Hitler though (I won't say where) and when I asked him if I could slip into the FastTrack lane and told him why he actually said to me, 'Come along now, sir. I hear this sort of thing all the time and I don't believe a word of it. You'll have to stay in line like everyone else.'

I really was suffering by this point but instead of clocking him one I just said, 'Thanks for fuck all, mate,' and then I got back in line. However, apparently you're not allowed to say the word 'fuck' to scroats like that so once I'd walked through the metal detector I was stopped by a load of guards who all but strip-searched me. In fact, the only thing they didn't do was stick a finger up my arse. If they had, they'd have had to cancel all flights.

Why can't you just keep your fucking mouth shut? I thought to myself. In my defence, though, it was four o'clock in the morning, I was getting asked for selfies and autographs left, right, and centre, and I was in a tremendous amount of pain.

That too is something that is part and parcel of being a strongman and if I don't wake up in the morning experiencing some kind of pain or soreness I know that I haven't been training hard enough. It's as simple as that. I'm not talking about a muscle strain or a twisted ankle. I'm talking about your entire body telling you to fuck off constantly. Even as I'm writing this, my back's throbbing like you wouldn't believe and I've got shooting pains going down my left arm. Anybody else would be running to A&E if they had this but if you're a strongman it's as normal as getting a hard on, but not nearly as much fun.

There's a part in my documentary where Geoff Capes reels off all the injuries he's had over the years and what he suffers from today, and it's a truly frightening list. This is on top of the usual stuff like strains, pulls and tears, by the way. He's had a new hip, operations on his knees, abdominal operations, problems with his vertebra and compressed nerves on his spine. Geoff finishes his litany of injuries by saying, 'Basically, I'm buggered,' and although it's quite a funny moment, he means it. He really is buggered.

The pain probably started when I was about fifteen or sixteen, and, like everything, it's just amplified as I've become bigger. Think about it. I'm ripping my muscles on a daily basis and so my body's usually awash with lactic acid.

Anyway, let's get on this plane to the World's Strongest Man competition in China.

As I said, I almost ended up killing a teacher on this flight, but with very, very good reason. The man was a disgusting arsehole and how the hell he ended up in charge of a load of children I'll never know.

We didn't get off to the best of starts because when I asked him – very nicely, I might add – if he'd mind swapping seats so that I could have the aisle seat he just shook his head once and didn't even look at me. This was a fourteen-hour flight we were about to embark on and even though there were just two of us in these seats, I was the one with my shoulder pushed up against the side of the plane with no bollock space and no room to stretch my legs. Teach, on the other hand, who was about three foot six inches tall, was free to stretch his legs out to touch the other side of the aisle, had they been long enough.

Chapter 21

The next thing this arsehole started doing was farting. I even said to him at one point, 'You dirty little bastard,' but I think he took that as a compliment.

Every single air mile bestowed on me a new level of hatred for man. Whenever he wanted to attract the stewardess's attention, instead of pushing the button or catching the stewardess's eye politely as she passed in the accepted manner, he'd shout and start waving his hand.

And few hours into the flight he started spitting in the aisle. I'm not talking about spitting out orange pips. This man was hoiking up greenies like you would not believe. None of the airline staff seemed to give a shit, by the way, which concerned me slightly.

By the time we reached Sanya I was capable of just about anything and when I got up to disembark the plane, my feet were the size of melons and my body felt like it'd been in a twelve-round boxing match. This obviously made my mood even worse so from the moment I got out of my seat until we started queueing at passport control I walked about an inch behind this dickhead and as well as growling at him I started telling him what I was going to do to him. Of course he knew full well that I was there and by the time we got to passport control he'd got up to a canter and was almost shitting himself. I'm afraid I can't really repeat what I said to him but put it this way, if words alone could kill a man he'd have turned inside out and then burst into flames.

Unfortunately, my travelling companion's behaviour seemed to be representative of the general population and if I'd been given a pound for every time I saw somebody gobbing in the street I'd have been able to get a private plane home.

My spirits were not lifted by the accommodation, when I finally arrived at it. It's changed now, fortunately, but at the time the organisation of the World's Strongest Man had room for improvement. Luckily, Giants Live, who now run the qualifying events for World's Strongest Man, including Europe's Strongest Man and Britain's Strongest Man, are starting to incentivise us. They are growing the sport and that's my biggest motivation too. One of the reasons Giants Live are able to do this is because they stage their events in arenas and the ticket money is used to remunerate the athletes, which obviously motivates us to do well. They also sell the TV rights to the competitions, which helps generate more money, and everybody is happy.

CHAPTER 22

Making a Big Impression in Hungary

Despite not getting through to the final at World's Strongest Man 2013, I only missed out by half a point, and as well as winning three events in my heat, I was first reserve for the final. So, within just a year of completely flunking World's Strongest Man and feeling totally out of my depth, I'd elevated myself to become the eleventh strongest man on the planet. Not bad, I guess. The improvement had been perfect really – steady and organic – and the only thing I was slightly disappointed about was the fact that it had taken me so long for the penny to drop so that I shifted my training from just weights, to weights and actual events. By now I'd invested in some serious strongman equipment, such as a yoke, a log and some atlas stones, and I'd also changed gyms. The place I was at originally was just a bog-standard gym that was part of a chain, whereas the new place, Strength Asylum, majors in things like strongman, powerlifting and bodybuilding. I've been there ever since. They allow me to keep all my equipment on-site which means I can train strongman events whenever I like. Except the truck pull, that is. For that I have to borrow a lorry from a local skip company (Jumbo Skips in Newcastle-under-Lyme) and then pull it around a trading estate. Oh, the glamour!

Speaking of glamour, it took me a total of thirty hours to get back to the UK from China and by the time I walked through my front door I was literally on my knees. It was great seeing Alex and the kids but I felt like a fucking zombie. The following morning I was due to catch a flight to Belfast to defend my UK's Strongest Man crown and as I got into bed that night I was ready to abdicate. Fuck me, was I tired. By the time I woke up, all thoughts of abdication had vanished and the only things running through my head were Alex, the kids, and thoughts about the next World's Strongest Man competition. It was now another year until the next tournament and if I wanted to see another improvement I'd have to get my head down. It was going to be tough but I was confident that within two years there would be four men vying for the title of World's Strongest Man, not three, and one of them would be a narky bearded twat from Stoke.

But for now my most pressing urgency was my home title to defend. By the time I boarded the plane for Belfast I was like a man possessed and was so confident in my abilities that I'm pretty sure I could have flown the plane myself. In fact, I know I could. I can fly a plane, by the way. It's a piece of piss.

Once again, I've watched a couple of recordings of this tournament and you can see I'm absolutely on the frigging money.

Very, very businesslike. I don't waste a drop of energy, so there's no showboating, and subsequently, I make mincemeat of the opposition. What actually helped was knowing that I was going to be tired. That made me sharp. This was my third UK's Strongest Man title on the bounce and although it wasn't the World's, it still felt fantastic. One thing I'd forgotten about until I watched the recording back was the fact that instead of winning a nice trophy like you would at most strongman events, you get a glass vase! I think they might have got them muddled up with a sewing competition or something. When the titles are running at the end of the show and I'm standing on the podium trying to look hard, you can't help noticing that instead of holding aloft a miniature statue of Charles Atlas or whatever, I'm trying to hide a nice piece of glassware.

Anyway, job done, so you'd think at this point I could relax slightly, right? Wrong. There was one more tournament in 2013, which was memorable for all the wrong reasons. As well as visiting Hungary for the first time, which was nice, I caused a diplomatic incident that had Colin Bryce apologising, not only to the Hungarian parliament, but also to the President himself.

I know you're not surprised but I'm going to tell you anyway.

This was a Giants Live event, which meant it was also a qualifier for the Worlds, and the two big names in attendance were me and the American, Mike Burke. Sure enough, Mike and I finished first and second respectively, but as opposed to just turning up, competing, and then pissing off again, like we normally did, we were invited by the sports minister to go on a tour of the Hungarian houses of parliament. As well as being a fan of strongman, this man was also a two-time Olympic champion and because Colin had said that it would be rude to refuse the invitation I reluctantly agreed. It's not that I didn't want to go (honest!), I just hated being on my feet for too long and it just wasn't my kind of thing. But because my mentor said it was the right thing to do, I grabbed my bum bag and off we went.

I have to say that this sports minister guy was really welcoming and the first ten minutes or so were actually quite interesting. After that it all became a bit boring and by the time we reached the chamber where the National Assembly of Hungary sits I was looking for a distraction. Luckily, or unluckily if you're Hungarian or Colin Bryce, a large group of Japanese tourists suddenly appeared in the chamber and without even thinking I ran off down the stairs and made my way to what turned out to be the President's lectern; somewhere only the President is allowed to go. In order to get to the lectern I had to pass two very heavily armed guards but as I approached them at speed their jaws just dropped, so instead of getting shot, I got through. It was all going well so far and now I'd caught the Japanese tourists' attention I was determined to give them a show.

As soon as I got to the lectern I ripped off my vest and started a full posing routine, showing off all the different muscle groups. The poor sports minister was in a state of shock by this time but the Japanese tourists were lapping it up and all you could hear, apart from the odd gasp, were cameras going off. It was straight out of *Pumping Iron*, really. Very professional.

Not being an actual bodybuilder, I eventually ran out of poses, but because my public wanted more, I decided to give them more. *I know,* I thought. *I'll do a Usain Bolt pose. That's quite current.*

Within a second I was attempting what I thought was an Usain Bolt pose, but because I hadn't got it quite right the Hungarian sports minister and virtually everyone else there, apart from Colin and the Japanese, mistook it for a Nazi salute. When Colin realised what the sports minister and gathered dignitaries were all thinking he shat his pants and he still describes it as 'that awful, awful moment'. You don't have to be a historian to know that Hungary was once invaded by the Nazis and although time's obviously a great healer the last thing they were expecting was an unintentional reminder via a topless strongman at the President's lectern. It was not one of my greatest moments and as well as writing several letters of apology, Colin also had to speak directly to the President. Fortunately for me, one of our cameramen had been filming the tour and so we were able to prove that it definitely wasn't a Nazi salute, just a crude Usain Bolt pose.

I really do think we should move on now. Certainly out of Hungary!

CHAPTER 23
Doncaster to L.A.

Although every year has been pivotal in its own way, 2014 was make or break and it's the closest I've ever come to jacking it all in. Up until then I'd always been what you'd call an enthusiastic amateur, I suppose, which is what the majority of strongmen still are. There are a few full-time professionals, but although there aren't many there were enough then to keep me from getting my hands on the only trophy I genuinely dreamt about winning. Remain an enthusiastic amateur and the best I could ever hope for, realistically, was a domestic trophy or two and a finals place at World's Strongest Man. Not a podium though. In order to achieve that I would need to become a professional but to become a professional I would need sponsors who were willing to give me cash.

Those sorts of negotiations were beyond me so what I actually needed more than anything was a manager. But where do I get a ...? You get the picture. It was all a bit overwhelming. For the time being, I had to put these thoughts on hold but they were very much in the back of my mind as I entered my next competitions.

Chapter 23

The year got off to a fantastic start as it marked my first ever win at Britain's Strongest Man, which is the UK's longest running and most prestigious competition. The first man to win it back in 1979 was the great Geoff Capes and since then two other World's Strongest Man winners, Gary Taylor and Jamie Reeves, had won the competition plus my two mates, Terry Hollands and Laurence Shahlaei. The competition had taken a break between 2009 and 2011 and after Laurence dominated the first two years back it was my turn to take over. It might not be an international trophy but Britain's Strongest Man is one of the sport's biggest domestic competitions, and with a qualification place for World's Strongest Man up for grabs I was desperate to show my dominance.

The competition took place on March 16 at the Doncaster Dome and the events were as follows:

1. Farmer's walk and duck walk medley (130kg–140kg (286–308 lb) farmer's; 200kg (441 lb) duck walk – 20 metres each)
2. Log lift for reps – 150kg (331 lb)
3. Deadlift for reps – 340kg (750 lb)
4. Dumbbell for reps – 100kg (220 lb)
5. Conan's Wheel
6. Loading race – sacks and barrels

There were nine competitors from Great Britain in total: Terry Hollands, Laurence Shahlaei, Mark Felix, Graham Hicks, Ben

Kelsey, Lloyd Renals, Simon Jonston, Brian Irwin and myself. Plus there were a further three international competitors: Kevin Larsen from Norway, Marco Guidi from Italy and Daniel Garcia from Gibraltar. Not a soft line-up, by any means.

I finished up standing top middle on the podium with Graham Hicks to my right and Laurence Shahlaei to my left. In the athletes meeting prior to the competition all the athletes had kept calling out who they thought was going to win each event and, because they all seemed to be unanimous, and because they didn't mention me, it got under my skin. Not one person had me down for a single win so it was the perfect motivation. It's also why I gave Laurence Shahlaei the middle finger as I was completing the final event. Everybody had him down as the overall winner and I wasn't having any of it. It was a good day's work, all in all.

As the biggest win of my career this did my profile no harm whatsoever and when World's Strongest Man came along just a week or so later I had companies falling over themselves to sponsor me. The trouble was they were all offering kit as opposed to cash and, as much as I appreciated their support, it wasn't going to afford me the opportunity to achieve parity with the three professionals who all but ruled the sport: Thor Björnsson, Brian Shaw and Žydrūnas Savickas.

I know I keep banging on about money, incidentally, but I've always felt the need to shout about it. It was very simply a matter of survival at the beginning. But as I've gradually become a bigger box office draw, it's become more about realising my worth and getting my fair share.

I did a few seminars a couple of years ago and I remember somebody asking me what the prize money was for World's Strongest Man. When I told them the winner got $45,000 I could see their jaws dropping. 'Is that all?' they said. 'You easily could earn that doing a normal job.' You can see why cash sponsorship was a necessity.

Despite the difficulties with turning pro still hanging over my head, my immediate goal was to focus on reaching the finals of World's Strongest Man. When I arrived in Los Angeles for the qualifiers I was bigger and stronger than I'd ever been. In fact, I was almost the finished article. A good performance here and perhaps some cash might materialise.

In the very first event I managed to injure my right bicep when picking up a sack but fortunately it wasn't serious. Even so, I still finished that event last and already had my work cut out. Once again, I've watched this heat back and for some reason I seem to be on my best behaviour. There isn't quite so much bravado as normal and I even wish one of the other competitors luck, which isn't like me. To be honest I think the injury made me nervous and because I'd come so close the year before I think I was feeling the pressure a bit. Fortunately, as the heat progressed, I gained confidence and ended up finishing second behind

Jerry Pritchett, who was the man I'd wished luck. The only reason I didn't win the group was because I didn't need to. First and second went through and by the time we got to the atlas stones I'd done enough. What mattered was that, at the third time of asking, I was at last through to the final of World's Strongest Man.

The first event of the final took place on the beautiful Venice Beach … but that's where the positives end, I'm afraid. It was a loading race – three huge tyres weighing 100kg each – and the thing that scuppered me was not only my technique, but also the fact that we were having to carry these things on sand. Just walking on sand is hard enough but when you're trying to run while carrying a massive tractor tyre it tends to present problems. Each of us had our own technique and unfortunately mine was shit. Unlike everyone else, who tried to carry it over their shoulder, I decided to get inside the tyre and then carry it like some enormous hula hoop, but as hard as I tried to remain upright I just kept on falling arse over tit. It had worked in the familiarisation session! One event down and out of a field of twelve I lay last on one point. Oh dear. Actually, oh bollocks!

The next event, the circus medley which is axle press and circus dumbbell, was a slight improvement and I ended up finishing mid-table. This left me ninth overall which was, quite frankly, appalling, but highlighted perfectly the gulf that existed between me and the top three (the rest didn't matter). I so wanted to be in that club.

The next event, which was the keg toss, demonstrated not only the top tier's dominance, but also how being a lanky freak like Brian or Thor can give you an advantage at certain events. That's taking nothing away from their strength, by the way. It's just a fact. Even so, their performances were absolutely astonishing and I came away half wanting to ask for their autographs, and half wanting to kill them. I should have killed them really!

You had two throw eight kegs in all over a bar – two at 40 lb, two at 45 lb, two at 50 lb and two at 55 lb – and the bar was set at six metres. Brian Shaw stepped up and did all eight in just under seventeen seconds. This performance was just astounding and when Brian stood on the sidelines waiting to watch Thor he must have thought he had it in the bag. I say in the documentary that Thor's like a kid who's been locked in a shed for twenty-six years and then released, and that's absolutely bob on. He chucked all eight of those kegs in 16.35 seconds and if you're wondering if that's fast, just you try picking up twenty or thirty kilograms and then imagine having to throw it over six metres in the air. You'd have to do it eight times, of course. The look on Brian's face was an absolute picture and we were all saying the same thing, basically: how in the name of Odin's arse did you do that?

The final three events told a similar story as far as I was concerned, and because of a litany of errors (all of which I learned from), I would only excel in one of them. That was the squat lift and the only man who managed to beat me was the eventual winner, Žydrūnas Savickas. Once again, I finished mid-table and despite being envious of what I was witnessing I was learning a massive amount. I went home to Stoke hungrier than ever to go professional and start realising my true potential.

CHAPTER 24

Deadlift Drama

I had almost five months until the next big event and spent all of that time either mending trucks, training, eating, sleeping or looking for sponsors and which meant I had precious little time for the wife and kids. This is a running theme throughout this book and gets a whole lot worse later on. Even though we'd been married just a couple of years, Alex's patience was already starting to run thin and it's not difficult to see why. My excuse for being AWOL was that I was doing it for her and the kids and that once I'd won World's Strongest Man everything would be different. That's all good and well when you're starting out but once reality sets in it can turn sour. Despite all my promises, I think Alex was having difficulty seeing the light at the end of the tunnel. To me there was no doubt I was going to get there but there's only so many times you can say to somebody, 'It won't be like this forever, I promise.'

One thing that I hoped would instil some belief in Alex was Europe's Strongest Man and in particular the world deadlift championships, which was the warm-up event. As somebody who excelled at the deadlift this was the chance for me to bag a world record, which once again would heighten my profile and enable me to get closer to my ambition.

The venue for both these competitions was Headingley Rugby Stadium and with an audience of 5,000-plus – and, as the current holder of the title of Britain's and UK's Strongest Man – I knew that the crowd would be right behind me.

The night before I hardly got a wink of sleep as I was a bit nervous but I actually got out of bed feeling OK, I'm not advocating insomnia as an aid for achieving success but sometimes it can help sharpen the mind and body and fortunately this was one of these occasions.

The deadlift world record is the only one that really matters in strongman, as despite being a relatively simple exercise it's the one that uses all the muscle groups and exemplifies what strongmen do: see who can lift the most weight. I'd smashed it in the gym on several occasions and was itching for the opportunity to make it mine.

The first round was 400kg (881 lb) (the current world record was 460kg (1,013 lb) and I pulled it as a speed rep. Benedikt 'Benni' Magnússon also did well but I was the only one who pulled it like a toy. By the way, it wasn't that long ago that 400kg would have been a new world record so this demonstrates just how far strongman has come over the past ten years or so. Or, if you want a more exact marker, since I came on the scene.

If you watch it on the documentary there's no strain whatsoever on that initial lift and I stomp off the platform like a man possessed. It was one of the first times I remember actually feeding off a crowd and the moment I locked it out they went mad. Because it had been so easy they knew what was coming and the energy they were creating was like having an extra limb.

Next up was 420kg (925 lb), which is when we started having one or two casualties. That was to be expected as a lot of the athletes wanted to save themselves for the main event, but in my case, this *was* the main event.

Round three was up to 435kg (959 lb) and about an inch before locking it out I tripped backwards and dropped the bar. Fortunately, I still had time to go again but from an 'energy expended' point of view it meant I was one lift ahead of everyone else. Even so, I still pulled it and in doing so managed to set a new British record. This, again, is when I noticed the incredible power of the crowd and when I locked out the lift I stood there, soaking it all in, and even gestured to sports presenter Caroline Pearce and the Channel 5 film crew up to come and have a word with me. Well, if you're going to showboat you may as well do it on camera – *and* while giving an interview.

By the end of round three, Loz Shahlaei had matched my record 435kg and so going into round four we had me; Loz; Benni Magnússon; the Austrian, Martin Wildauer; and Yorkshireman Andy Bolton, who was the first man ever to deadlift a thousand pounds. The weight we were attempting was 445kg (981 lb).

Unfortunately, Loz tore his lat while attempting his lift and, with Wildauer and Bolton not getting anywhere near, that just left Benni and I. Because I'd done the extra lift everybody thought I'd be exhausted, and, given the amount of sleep I'd had (or hadn't had), perhaps I should have been. Tired or not, I walked onto that platform swimming in confidence and with the help of about one hundred and ten decibels of noise I lifted that bar in about two seconds flat. Once I'd locked it out and referee Magnús Ver Magnússon's hand had gone down, I suddenly felt a swathe of what can only be described as industrial-strength joy flooding through my body and as the crowd stood up and went mental I just stood there with the lift locked out and shouted, 'Oh *fuck* yeah!' Watch the documentary and read my lips. It's not difficult! What an unbelievable feeling.

Next up was 461kg (1,016 lb), which would be a new world record – the heaviest weight anybody had ever lifted in the history of the world. For the last few years Benni had dominated the deadlift scene and although he was still obviously one of the best I knew I could do him. I just knew it. He was at the height of his powers whereas I was improving all the time.

Benni went up first for the record and despite struggling midway through for a few seconds he pulled it relatively quickly and, more importantly, he pulled it cleanly. As much as I don't like seeing Benni pull world records, watching his reaction was a treat. Because he's Icelandic I have no idea what the fucking hell he's saying, but once he puts the bar down he jumps forward and starts screaming at the bloody audience.

Now it was my turn. Taking to the platform, all I could hear in front of me were the crowd shouting, 'Come on, Eddie.' It was almost as if all 5,000 of them were taking it in turns with each one being a bit too impatient to wait for the other to finish. The lift itself was a different animal to the others and represented a massive jump. This was necessary, as going up by two or three kilograms would have taken about ten bloody lifts.

As I started to raise the bar I knew I had enough in the tank but it was going to be close. *Just pick the fucking thing up, Eddie*, I thought. *You cannot let him beat you.* Once it was at the top of my thighs I knew I had done it and all in all it took me about six seconds to lock it out, which isn't too shabby really. As I did so the noise just got louder and louder but there was going to be no showboating this time. All I wanted to see was Magnus's hand go down so I could claim my share of the record. It seemed to take an age but eventually it did, which meant the lift was good. I may only have had a share of a world record, I thought. But it was better than nothing.

And then it happened.

In what I can only describe as being a last-minute attempt at showmanship I dropped the bar, and the moment I did so Magnus put his arm back out, and waved it once from left to right. That meant disqualification.

I must have watched this back a thousand times (I really must be a glutton for punishment!) and the look on my face says it all. It was as though life itself had come to an end very,

very abruptly and I remember experiencing a pang of desperation. It was almost like an electric shock.

The night before at the athletes' meeting, Magnus, who was the chief referee, had said, 'I want you to lower the bar, don't drop it,' and to be honest, I just don't think I was listening. Rule or no rule, what fucked me off at the time was that it made no difference to the lift itself and so, as there was so much riding on it, why not just give me the lift? It was a good lift, so why not? In hindsight, yes of course I should have listened and put the fucking bar down nicely but situations like this are what make me so incredibly fascinating. Rightly or wrongly, I felt enormously aggrieved straight after the lift and as well as shedding a few tears I also shouted one or two naughty words into something that looked suspiciously like a microphone. Once again, I'd like to apologise for that as there were kids present but there was so, so much riding on that lift. To have it taken away from me *after* I'd locked it out was the ultimate kick in the dick.

In an interview in the physio room afterwards I said that I didn't really care about the disqualification and that in my eyes I was still a world record holder. I even said I was happy! But that was just me trying to save face. At the end of the day, I'd fucked up big time and what happened afterwards, which was a bout of full-blown depression, wasn't nice for anyone.

The last time I'd experienced what I consider to be a true period of depression, as opposed to the downer I go on after a competition, was when my nan had been suffering from leukaemia, and unfortunately this was pretty damn close to that. I felt destroyed inside and for a week or two afterwards I could hardly bring myself to speak to anybody. Even Alex. She and I are a partnership and I suppose I felt like I'd let her and the kids down. Worst of all, I was starting to have feelings of self-doubt. It didn't matter how much Alex or my parents believed in me, if *I* didn't think I could do it any more I knew I may as well just jack it in right now.

It's actually quite childish in a way but the epicentre of my resentment was having the record for a few seconds and then having it taken away from me. It was like a toddler having its toy snatched off him. If I'd failed the lift I'd still have had the motivation to come back and do it again but because I'd already done it, that motivation had been replaced by sadness and indignation. And they're not the emotions you really need when you're about to lift heavy weights!

After remaining silent for a week or so, Alex sat me down for a chat. It wasn't that I didn't want to speak to her, I just didn't feel able to. Even so, I wasn't required to say a word on this occasion as she was the one doing the talking. Her rallying call, which was exactly what I needed, went something like this:

'Have you any idea what you achieved at Headingley a couple of weeks ago? Any idea at all? You, together with Benni, lifted more weight than any other person who has ever walked the Earth. Do you know how amazing that is? You always talk about wanting to be the best, but the fact of the matter is, you already are! Don't you realise that, Eddie, you already are the best in the world. Dropping the bar was unfortunate but it shouldn't affect your strength, physical or mental. The Eddie I know would learn from this, take the positives and come out fighting. Don't allow this to spoil your career, Eddie. Please!'

As Alex had started talking I'd been slumped on the sofa, which is where I'd been for the last two weeks. I was only really half listening at first but after a few seconds something inside me clicked and the more she talked the more it seemed to make sense. By the time Alex said the words 'come out fighting', I was sitting bolt upright on the sofa and with a bit of warming up I could probably have lifted 470kg (1,036 lb) there and then.

'God, you're right,' I said. 'What the fuck have I been doing?'

'Never mind that. Just go out there and do what you do best.'

For the last two weeks, I'd felt like the most badly served person in the world, yet in fact I was one of the luckiest. More importantly, I was also one of the strongest people in the world – potentially *the* strongest – and it was time to start making people aware of that fact.

CHAPTER 25

Mighty Mo

The biggest priority now in my attempt for world domination was to get the freedom, and the cash, to go pro. And so, as opposed to moping around the house feeling sorry for myself and getting on everyone's tits, I hit the gym and started putting myself about in front of Stoke's business community.

The first event I attended was a charity darts match at Stoke City's stadium in October 2014. The former World Darts Champion Adrian Lewis was taking part, as were several members of the football team, and as I was a local celebrity I'd been invited. Fortunately for me the organisers had asked if they could introduce me to the crowd and ask me a few questions and given what I was after, I obviously agreed. As a shop window this event was invaluable, as in addition to me probably being unknown to quite a few of the people present, there was enough money in the room to raise the *Titanic*.

Sure enough, as I walked onto the stage most of the room seemed to gasp and before the MC started speaking, all I could hear were people saying things like, 'Look at the size of him!' and 'Is he that the strongman who's been on TV?'

It was an ideal situation really and so in order not to bugger things up I decided not to swear.

Unbeknownst to me, sitting in the room that night was a local businessman called Mo Chaudry. He owns WaterWorld in Stoke which is the largest waterpark in the UK, and, as well as once appearing on Channel 4's *Secret Millionaire*, he'd also advised the great Phil Taylor at the start of his career. More importantly, Mo's father, who had moved to the UK from Pakistan in the 1960s, had once been an old-fashioned stone-lifting strongman and even Mo himself had been a powerlifter and a weightlifter at university and had been a medallist at the British student championships. According to him, he was quite taken aback when he saw me at the event but because he was entertaining guests he never got a chance to say hello.

Fast forward a few months and I was at a spa and fitness club I'd recently joined in Newcastle called M-Club. I use the place for swimming mainly, but also some rehabilitation. One day the manager came in and said that the owner of M-Club would like to set up a meeting with me and when I asked why he was a bit vague. To cut a long story short, the owner in question was Mo and he's since admitted to me that one of the reason he wanted to see me was because he was afraid I'd scare his customers away. Charming! I think he was worried I'd be utilising the gym and was having visions of me using his customers as dumbbells. He needn't have worried. As much as I love going to M-Club, the gym is a bit, how do I say, underequipped for me.

Once Mo was satisfied that his customers weren't going to be used as weights, we started talking about my career. Without me even telling him that I was intending to go professional, he said that it would be essential if I ever wanted to progress.

'I saw you on TV over Christmas on *World's Strongest Man*,' he said. 'Do you know the difference between you and the big three? Apart from them being professional?'

'No,' I replied.

'You're in awe of them,' he said. 'I could tell by the way you looked at them.'

This bloke was sharp. I was in awe of Žydrūnas, Brian and Thor, as well you know, but nobody but me had ever noticed before.

'So, Eddie,' said Mo. 'How are you going to become the World's Strongest Man?'

'By going professional,' I replied.

'And how are you going to do that?'

'God only knows,' I said. 'I've got plenty of sponsorship opportunities. The problem is, none of them are offering cash.'

'OK,' said Mo. 'If you go professional, do you honestly think you could win World's Strongest Man?'

'Without any doubt,' I replied. 'All I need is a chance.'

Mo paused for a few seconds and then smiled.

'All right then,' he said. 'I'm going to give it to you.'

'What do you mean?' I said. I was feeling a bit slow that day.

'I'm going to sponsor you,' said Mo. 'I'm going to underwrite everything. Your mortgage, your bills, everything. I'll look for sponsors first, but if they don't materialise I'll pay for everything myself. How does three years sound? Will that be enough time?'

This all happened within about fifteen minutes.

'Well, yes,' I said, completely and utterly stunned. 'That should fine.'

'You've inspired me, Eddie,' Mo said. 'As far as I'm concerned you can hand in your notice at work first thing tomorrow morning.'

Because this had all happened so quickly I was honestly worried he hadn't thought it through properly.

'But what about living expenses?' I asked. 'It's not just a case of covering my bills.'

'I realise that,' he said. 'You work out exactly how much you need and I'll sort it,' he said.

It was an incredible offer but this is so typical of the guy. As with Colin Bryce, he just wanted to help me from the off and because of that I never once felt exploited. It was all about what he could do for me, not what I could do for him. It was the very opposite approach of how it felt with the World Class Potential Programme back in my swimming days.

However, a few days later when I went to Mo's office to sign the contract, I said, 'I'm sorry, Mo. I really appreciate your offer but I'm afraid I'm not going to sign this.'

'Why ever not, Eddie?' said Mo, quite rightly flabbergasted.

'Because I want you to represent me, as well as sponsor me,' I said.

The look on Mo's face was a picture. It went from extreme shock to out-and-out confusion in about two seconds.

'What do you mean you want me to represent you?' he said.

'Just that,' I replied. 'I want you to manage me. I've done some research on you and I've come to the conclusion that you're the best person to take me to the top.'

Before going to his office to sign I'd asked a lot of people about Mo and each and every one of them had said just that. He's the best person to take you to the top. Remaining self-contained was important to me – but as a strongman, not as a businessman. I was about to become a professional and I knew full well that as I progressed my profile would grow, as would the opportunities. I needed somebody to manage all that so I could concentrate on getting strong. In that respect, I was in the same situation as before I met Mo, just a step up.

'What do you think?' I said to him.

There was a pause.

'OK then,' he replied. 'Let's have an adventure.'

CHAPTER 26

Occupation: Strongman

I was now one of a very small and elite group of people: a professional strongman. It's not an occupation you see advertised down the job centre very often and, as I think you'll have gathered, it's not exactly a structured career. Everything I know about what it takes to be a top athlete in this event is what I've taught myself. So what does life as a professional strongman actually involve?

Well, first off, you have to eat a lot. And I mean *a lot*.

Many people dream about being able to eat as much food as they like but for me that's a reality. The only difference is that I don't dream about it. I have nightmares.

Last week alone I spent over £300 on food (that's for me alone) and I'll be doing the same thing every week now until I get to World's Strongest Man. That's my life. I sleep, I eat, I train and I recover. There's little deviation. But what would you say the most taxing of the four is?

Well, it's certainly not sleep. Saying that, due to my size I do have something called sleep apnea, which can result in me stopping breathing while I'm asleep. To help combat this I have to wear a CPAP mask in bed and although it's not ideal I wouldn't consider it to be an issue.

Training too, whilst being hard work, is over and done with in about four hours and because of the sense of achievement I get, I could hardly describe it as being taxing. I do get a bit bored of it sometimes and on some days I find it hard to go. Once I'm there, though, it's fine and at the end of the day it constitutes about 95 per cent of my social life.

Recovery is probably easier than sleeping really, apart from some of the physio, and because that's so pro-active that also give me a light sense of achievement. So, the most taxing aspect of my everyday life as a strongman is definitely food. You see, when I'm not eating the food, I'm buying it, and when I'm not buying the food, I'm researching how I can improve my diet. Seriously, brothers and sisters, consuming what I do really is all-consuming.

With food, like training, it's all about consistency, and if you miss a meal, believe it or not, you won't be as hungry for your next meal. It's all about keeping an equilibrium and if there's one thing a stomach doesn't like, it's surprises.

If you think all this eating doesn't leave me much time for anything else, you'd be right. People often ask me what hobbies I do in my spare time, but the fact of the matter is I don't have any hobbies, or any spare time. Remember what

I said earlier about having never been on any benders with the lads? Well, it's exactly the same with hobbies. And holidays, come to think of it. Alex and I have been together seven years now and we have never had a holiday. We didn't even have a honeymoon. That's pretty appalling when you think about it, but since we've been together I've hardly had time to breathe, let alone pack my bags and go and relax for a couple of weeks.

The closest I've ever come to having a hobby is when I called in at a fishing shop in Hanley about six or seven months ago and bought myself a fishing rod, some tackle and some bait. The intention was to grab a couple of hours each week (which you'd think would be doable) but it's all still in the boot of my car and will probably be there forever. It's a shame really as I was looking forward to giving it a go, but the fact is that while I'm competing at this level my life is not my own. That's just the way it is. What makes that worse is that my life doesn't belong to Alex or the kids either, and sometimes I'll spend no more than a couple of hours with them in a week. The only connection I have with normality is watching television, as boring as that sounds. That's what I do to relax and that's what I do when I spend time with my kids. Usually I'm too knackered to do anything else, and so, rightly or wrongly, it ticks an awful lot of boxes.

Horror films are my thing and if ever I do have an hour or two to myself I'll stick on a zombie film or an episode or two of *The Walking Dead*. Basically, anything with an apocalyptic theme to it. A lot of people equate watching films and television to escapism, and it's the same for me. The difference is that I like escaping to what might be the end of the world as opposed to a school full of fucking wizards. Where I get that from I have no idea, but it seems to suit my personality. I think I must be addicted to adversity (or is it aggro?), because it's a running theme with everything I do.

As for the training, most of it is done in the gym, of course, but I still do swim whenever I can. I normally go to the pool at least once a week, usually on a Sunday afternoon, and I do what's called HIIT training, where I try to keep my heart rate above 150 beats per minute for about fifty minutes. The way I do that is to do two twenty-five-metre lengths in the pool at a very fast pace. It usually takes me about forty seconds to do two lengths. Then I'll have about one minute and twenty seconds' rest. As that time comes to an end, when my heart rate's dropping to about 145 to 150, I go again. This way I'm always keeping my heart rate above 145 to 150 for fifty minutes. That increases your cardiovascular system massively. It also helps mobility in my shoulders and my spine.

As I said earlier, swimming keeps me mobile and that's why I'm one of the most flexible guys in strongman. Even at thirty-plus stone I can still get my palms on the floor without bending my legs and with the overhead events I can get my hands behind my head to press, no problem. A lot of my opponents can't do this because they're too muscle-bound, but I've found swimming has prevented that from happening to me. I still do mostly freestyle but if I get to a point where I'm really out of breath, I'll perhaps do a bit of breaststroke to recover a bit quicker. I can still swim fifty metres in under thirty seconds, which, if I do say so myself, is fucking impressive.

But of course it's the gym where I spend what feels like the majority of my life so I thought I'd finish off this chapter with a few stories about life in the gym, including the time my eyeball popped out. This part is not for the faint-hearted so if you're a bit sensitive it's probably best to move on.

I dread to think how many hours I've spent in the gym over the years but a rough estimate would be about 10,000 hours, which is just over a year. Bearing in mind I've only been going to the gym for the last fourteen years, that's a significant amount of time, and to be honest I've experienced all kinds of stuff there. Some of it good, some of it bad, some of it disturbing, and some of it painful. Let's face it, it's the last two you're most interested in so without further ado let me tell you the full story of how my eyeball popped out.

I would have been about eighteen or nineteen years old at the time and was pushing a thousand kilos on a leg press. Because I was always at the gym, my mates would often drop in to see me and on this particular day I was feeling a bit cocky.

'Why don't you sit on the leg press?' I said to two mates, which they did. 'Right, watch this, lads,' I said to the remaining group. 'I will now push a thousand kilos plus these two dickheads.'

Being a bit of a showman (or should I say show-off?), I decided to do the whole screaming and grimacing bit. The vast majority of this was obviously for effect, but what I also did was keep my eyes wide open which you're not supposed to do. Always keep your eyes squinted or even closed when you either lift or push, I'd always been told, but because I was young, naïve and knew better than everybody else this obviously didn't apply to me.

After four reps I was on the verge of winning an Oscar but then on the fifth something happened. When I say it was all for show, what I mean is that I was just exaggerating everything but in actual fact it was a bloody big weight. This was going to be my final rep but before I could lock it out I heard a popping sound from my right eye socket and then felt my eyeball pushing hard against my eyelids. I didn't feel any pain exactly but I knew something was up and so let down the weight as quick as I could.

Visually, this injury was on a par with something out of *Zombie Flesh Eaters* and the reaction of my mates was hilarious.

'OH MY GOD!' they all screamed as they ran away. 'YOUR EYE'S COME OUT! EDDIE, YOUR FUCKING EYE'S COME OUT!'

I was used to looking in the mirror as I trained but that was normally to admire my incredible physique and boyish good looks. Recoiling in horror was something I hadn't really anticipated but that was exactly what was happening. Fuck me, I looked strange. Very carefully I started pushing my eyeball back in but once it was there I couldn't see a damn thing.

'It's just dark,' I said to my mates, who had crept back to watch in appalled fascination.

'Don't worry,' they reassured me. 'It'll come back. Why don't you go again?'

Honestly, only a lunatic would take medical advice from this lot.

'Yeah, fuck it,' I said. 'Come on, somebody get back on.'

It took about two hours for my sight to come back but because I was young and daft I just assumed it would. I also did about three more sets and all in all it wasn't a bad workout. To be honest, it's not a story I used to tell very often for the simple reason that it only happened once and its novelty value in the gym lasted no longer than about ten minutes. It was only when somebody asked me about my mishaps in the gym that it came to mind, so I mentioned the story in my documentary and it's been a favourite ever since.

A far more common occurrence when training weights (usually when you're doing things like leg presses and squats) is shitting yourself. We've all done it at some stage. In fact, you could say it's the original rite of passage. I bet you're really glad I've mentioned this.

There is actually an art to keeping everything in while you're mid-rep but it's one that doesn't come easily, so to speak. The most dangerous time for me when it comes to shitting my pants is when I'm on the way back up from a squat, which is ironic really, as in the confines of a toilet that usually means I've just had one. The trick is to listen to your body, and the more you listen, the more you know when you need to go. It's just like training in that respect.

Something less messy but far more dangerous is passing out, and, once again, the art to practising prevention both begins and ends by listening to your body. Oh yes, and breathing! You have to remember to breathe.

The first time I ever passed out I was doing front squats. I had a bar across the front of my shoulders with my arms crossed holding the bar in and I think I had five plates on each side. Once again, I'd have been about eighteen or nineteen, which is when I started lifting heavier weights, and after doing about four reps the next thing I remember is waking up on my back. I don't remember feeling dizzy or anything. All I remember is waking up on my back with my legs folded behind me at the knees and the bar across my neck. Basically, I'd folded myself in half!

I think this was probably down to technique, or lack of it; I must have been resting the weight on my neck. This meant I was impeding some of my main arteries and so after a while I just went. That was seriously fucking scary! The thing is, you have to be so, so careful lifting weights, which is why I've included a list of dos and don'ts in this book for anybody who isn't sure. All I would add to that list is: if you're ever unsure whether you're doing anything right or if something doesn't feel right, for God's sake, stop what you're doing and ask! Be cocky and confident by all means, but make sure you use it to your advantage.

I've also passed out during deadlifts a few times, and, as with me shitting myself, it always happens on the way up. Actually, with a deadlift, it usually happens at the very end of the rep.

It doesn't matter what I'm lifting, I always hold my breath for maximum stability and sometimes that's my downfall. Yet again, it's all about listening to your body and so the longer you do this the more attuned you become to its needs and capabilities. Mark my words, I do not recommend anybody reading this book to hold their breath while they're lifting weights. To do so, you have to be completely in touch with your body (or as much as you can be) and even then, you are taking risks that may not be worth it.

All in all, then, being a professional strongman isn't a career that would suit anyone. It's only for those who really are prepared to sacrifice their life for their ambition, who have a burning drive to be the best and to challenge their body to the limit on a daily basis. Or just the nutcases, depending on how you want to look at it.

Anyway, back to the story. You want to know how Mo Chaudry's gamble on me worked out, don't you? Suddenly it seemed like even more was riding on my success …

CHAPTER 27

Attempting the Arnolds

Luckily for Mo – or, should I say, Mo's bank balance – he was able to find enough sponsors who were willing to pay me cash and I'm happy to say that each and every one of them has stayed with me. It's the perfect arrangement, really: they enable me to train full time and in return they get the best of me.

The first major international competition I entered after going pro was the Arnold Classic in America, Arnold Schwarzenegger's own strongman competition. If ever there was an event tailor-made for me to win, it was this. I mean, come on. How often have I mentioned Arnold Schwarzenegger in this book so far? Fucking loads! The man's a God to me and so to say I was looking forward to competing in his competition would be a gross understatement. But it was also intimidating – not because of the prospect of meeting my hero for the first time, although that did give me a few sleepless nights, the kind you have on Christmas Eve – no, it was because of the reputation of the competition itself. The Arnolds, as it's known, is widely considered to be the most challenging strongman contest on earth and although it doesn't have the cachet of World's Strongest Man it carries more prize money and is certainly the most intense.

The competition itself is part of the Arnold Sports Festival, a multi-sport event consisting of various competitions including professional bodybuilding (the Arnold Classic) and strongman (the Arnold Strongman Classic). Set up in the late 1980s, it's become one of the biggest sporting festivals on the planet and now has events all over the world.

What surprised me most of all were the amount of people there. Until then I'd been used to competing in front of, at most, five thousand, and when I first walked into the exhibition centre in Columbus, Ohio, it almost took my breath away. Apparently there are over a quarter of a million people who attend this event each year and a fair chunk of these are strongman fans.

I actually found the enormity of the event quite intimidating at first and I was completely out of my comfort zone. I just wasn't used to being around so many people. I soon adjusted to it though and when I was finally introduced to the crowd for the first time it was like being at the MGM Grand. The MC was pure Las Vegas!

'Our next competitor, from England – Eddie Hall! Twenty-seven years old, six foot three inches tall and weighing 385 lb. FOUR TIMES UK's Strongest Man!'

Each competitor has to walk on carrying their home nation flag and then stand in a line facing the audience. We do the same at all the Giant's Live events and it looks great.

Since 2003, Žydrūnas Savickas has won this title no fewer than eight times and behind him is Brian Shaw on three. A lot of people credit Žydrūnas as being the strongest man who's ever lived and after the first event on the first day I wouldn't have disagreed with them.

The event in question was the Austrian Oak, which is basically a log press (i.e. lifting a log-shaped bar above your head – not exactly easy as it's an awkward shape to hold), First up was Benni Magnússon. He had a good go but couldn't get the last ten inches. Up next was Thor and he barely got it above his head. This thing was fucking heavy, by the way: 405 lb (205kg)! After him was Brian Shaw, who didn't fare much better, and after two more disappointed hopefuls it was my turn. My first event at my first Arnold Classic. Nervous? I was crapping myself! There must have been at least 10,000 people there but as always I went out there with the intention of giving it absolutely everything.

Just getting this thing onto your chest takes up a massive amount of energy and by the time I was ready to push for a lift I already felt half gone. Even so I pushed for all I was worth and on my first attempt I was about the same as Benni. This wasn't good enough so because I still had time I decided to go again. This time it came up a bit easier and so without fannying around I went straight for the lift. I was literally about an inch away from locking it out but I just didn't have it in me. Bollocks! I certainly wasn't happy but that thing was just absolute immense.

Last up was Žydrūnas and because of his reputation everyone had stayed back to see if he could do it. Thor, Brian, me ... we were all standing by the side of the stage hoping he'd be having an off day. He wasn't. He walked onto the stage, picked it up like it was a fucking twig and then lifted it in about two seconds flat. I'd seen enough.

Next up was the frame walk, which was set on an incline, and once again I struggled for some reason. I can't put my finger on it. I just wasn't at the races.

When I got back to my hotel room that evening I was both pissed off and miffed. Finishing the first day in eighth after two of my best events was not a good start but tomorrow was another day. Thank God!

Fortunately, after having a good night's sleep and a bit of a word with myself I felt cracking the next day and arrived at the exhibition centre absolutely full of it. The first event was the tyre deadlift and after getting rid of the also-rans it was just me and Brian Shaw in the final. The best I managed was 1,111 lb but he pipped me by pulling 1,117 lb. It was an improvement on yesterday but I still didn't feel right.

Going into the final event I was in fourth place but five points off the lead. The event in question was the circus dumbbell and again, it should have been another strong event for me. I can't remember where I finished in the event itself but what I do remember is lining up at the end of the final day for the presentation. This time I was dreading hearing that MC's voice as I knew what he was going to say.

'In sixth place, Eddie Hall.'

You wanker!

I was now one of the few full-time professional strongmen in the world and this was just dog shit. I'd let myself down. The only surprise bigger than me finishing sixth was Thor finishing seventh, so at least I wasn't alone. I remember commiserating with the big man directly after the presentation and between the two of us we could have depressed a roomful of pissed-up monkeys. Brian fucking Shaw won the competition, the gangly American freak. I remember looking on at Brian as Arnold Schwarzenegger (yes, I know!) handed him the trophy and his cheque. The word 'envy' doesn't even come close to covering the emotions I felt at that moment, but if you tried adding things like resentfulness, anger and hatred to the list, you'd be about half way. I love Brian but at that moment in time I wanted to rip off his head and shit down his neck.

As I walked away from the exhibition centre in Columbus, Ohio, with my cheque for $6,000, I wondered if I would ever get to meet my hero. I'd managed to grab a quick photo with him at the competition but hadn't said a word to him and had simply been one of thousands. That wasn't my style at all. I wanted to impress Arnold and make him notice me. I wanted him to want to speak to me.

Thanks to Colin Bryce, a new world record and some very tired athletes, that opportunity would come a lot sooner than I thought.

CHAPTER 28
The Beast is Let Loose

The day after the Arnold Classic I got on a plane and flew to Melbourne for the Australian version of the same competition. It took three flights in all and after spending thirty hours in the air I finally arrived in Australia. The longest of the three flights, which lasted seventeen hours, was actually the most comfortable but even so I was in fucking bits by the time I arrived at the hotel and so was looking forward to having a couple of days' rest.

I arrived in Melbourne on the Friday and we weren't meant to be competing until 11 a.m. on Sunday. Then, right out of the blue, the promoter of the event told Colin Bryce, who was running the strongman competition, that the start had been moved forward to 11 a.m. on Saturday. The reason it had been moved was because Arnold Schwarzenegger was supposed to be attending the first event, which was the deadlift, and for some reason he was turning up a day early. To try to impress Arnold, this promoter had promised him a world record attempt at deadlift and by all accounts the great man was looking forward to it.

The problem this presented to Colin was finding somebody who was willing to go for the record. Everybody was obviously knackered from travelling and competing for deadlift to max in a standard strongman event is a lot different to going for a world record as not only is there a little bit more pressure involved, but the weight is obviously increasing. The first person Colin tried was Brian Shaw but he refused, as did everyone. It was hardly surprising, given the notice involved. This would have been about 11 p.m. and so just twelve hours before the attempt. I'd already spoken to Colin when I'd arrived and he knew how exhausted I was. Even so, he decided to give me a try.

'Yeah, I'll give it a go, mate,' I said. It must have been the jet lag.

The posters for the Arnold competitions always have a bodybuilder at the centre and because our sport was always seen as the poor relation I decided to help out. There was also the prospect of meeting my hero, of course, but my primary motivation, if I'm honest, was just to help out Colin.

The reason Arnold was interested in seeing a world record attempt at deadlift was because he himself used to be a powerlifter, which I wasn't aware of. According to Colin he'd pulled 720 lb (327kg) back in the late 1960s, which is some weight.

The following morning, at about 10.50 a.m., I was all ready to go. Actually that's a lie because I felt like shit. What I mean is that I'd just finished the main deadlift event and if I was going to go for a world record it would have to happen quickly. I'd actually had a shocker in the event, by the way, and had struggled on 360kg (793 lb). So how the fuck I was going to lift 462kg (1,018) was a mystery.

Then, all of a sudden, the promoter received a phone call from a rather doubtful Arnold Schwarzenegger. 'Are you sure you've got somebody who can pull 1,019 lb?' he said. 'With a real bar?'

'Yes,' said the promoter. 'And he has to lift now.'

'OK,' said Arnold. 'Hang on. I'll be there in five minutes.'

Thirty minutes later we're still sitting there like lemons and so in the end I said, 'Look, Colin. I'm getting cold now. I've got to go for it. At least let's give the crowd a bit of a show.'

The world deadlift record was still held by Benni Magnússon and you all know the history behind that. I knew I had to give it another go to lay to rest the demons from my disqualified previous attempt. Also Colin and the promoter were having a nightmare and so the least I could do was help them make the best of a bad job. I may not have had my hero there to watch me but I felt this was my chance to step up.

As I was psyching myself up, Colin received a text from Arnold. 'On my way,' it said.

'Eddie, Eddie, Eddie!' he screamed. 'Arnold's on his way. He'll be here any second.'

'OK, I'm ready,' I told him.

Arnold or no Arnold, by the time I got myself into position, I could see that Colin had done a fantastic job warming up the crowd. Because of the noise they were making I was starting to feel strong again. They were only standing just a few yards behind me and there was so much energy. I obviously didn't realise the significance of it then, but when Colin went to introduce me he said: 'From Stoke-on-Trent, to take the world record by one kilogram! Lifting 1019 lb! Eddie "THE BEAST" Hall!' It was the first time anyone had called me that. The moment he said it the crowd started chanting, 'Beast, Beast, Beast!' and as I locked on, put on my straps and the prepared to lift, that was all I could hear. Fuck me, I felt strong now. I felt like I'd had fifteen hours' kip.

Unbeknownst to me, just as I started lifting the bar, Arnold Schwarzenegger walked up with his entourage and although I wasn't aware of it he stood beside me and started shouting in my ear. There'd been doubt in my mind right up until a second or so into the lift but as I started to pull northwards I could actually feel myself getting stronger and stronger. Then before you could say, 'I need your clothes, your boots and your motorcycle,' I was standing with Arnold Schwarzenegger at my side having become the first man ever to lift 1,019 lb. Fucking get in there!

After putting – not dropping – the bar down, I took off my straps and went mental for a minute and as well as jumping around and shouting 'YES!' and 'AAAAARGH!' a lot, I screamed the word 'LIGHTWEIGHTS!', which was obviously directed at those athletes who'd chosen not to attempt the record. Sorry, but I just couldn't resist.

The first person to come up and congratulated me was Arnold – or Arnie, to his mates. He actually touched me! Which is surprising really, as I was covered in fucking sweat. The first thing he said was, 'Wow, you really are a beast!' and from then on, that was it – the name stuck. *Fuck the Spartan*, I said to myself. *If Arnold says I'm a beast, I'm a beast!*

I think I've had several 'best days of my life' in this book, but until the next one comes along I'm claiming this one to be it. I honestly couldn't believe it. The first time I'd noticed Arnold was present was when I'd almost locked out the lift. I suddenly saw these purple loafers to the right of me and I remember thinking, *Who the hell wears purple loafers?*

After congratulating me, Arnold interviewed me for the TV cameras and that was just astonishing. The first question he asked me was how much training I did, and so I told him that it was 365 days a year and then I explained what had happened at Headingley with the disqualification. By this time I was starting to well up because all I could think about was how close I'd come to jacking it all in, and all because of a disqualified lift. After what had just happened – and what was actually happening – that was one scary thought. The two people who'd had made this possible, apart from me, were Alex, who had persuaded me not to give up, and Mo Chaudry, who'd given me the opportunity to go full time.

Looking back, what I actually find equally scary is the thought of what might have happened had Magnus given me the lift. For starters I'd have shared the world record with Benni Magnússon, and I don't like sharing. What I find even more disturbing is the thought of me not having that hunger – that madness, even – that the disqualification eventually sparked after Alex had got through to me.

After telling Arnold my life story and explaining how I'd come back from the brink, he said, 'You're a winner, a champion, somebody who has failed in various different lifts, but every time you've got up again. That's what winners do. They don't stay down, they get up and they get going. Congratulations, and I hope you'll say [this is where I had to join in] – I'LL BE BACK!'

CHAPTER 29

Life in the Spotlight

That year, 2014, was the year I realised I was famous and I remember thinking to myself, *At last, some recognition!* By now I'd appeared on all kinds of TV shows (not only strongman) and it had got to the point where I was recognised pretty much everywhere I went. This was, and is, extremely gratifying for me, but I think the game changer in terms of being recognised was the advent of selfies. I used to have this notion when I was younger that if and when I ever became famous I'd be stopped and asked for an autograph or a chat. It never entered my head that I'd be asked to have my photo taken and I don't mind admitting that it took some getting used to. To make things simpler I decided to use just one pose, which I pull for all selfies regardless of who's taking it. And before you ask, no, it's not a Usain Bolt!

One of the only times I don't like having my photo taken is when I'm out with my family, which, as you know, is about as rare as rocking-horse shit. I also don't like being asked if I'm in pain, so don't ever ask me for a selfie if I'm standing in a queue at an airport! Generally speaking though, I love it, and what I like most of all is that people usually have something nice to say. That does make everything worthwhile some days, and it can make a big difference to how I feel. Some young lad coming up and saying, 'Hey Eddie, I'm a really big fan of yours,' can give you just enough encouragement to make it through to the following day. It really is that simple.

On the rare occasions when I refuse to have a selfie taken I'm called all kinds of names on social media and whoever's been refused will usually mutter something derogatory as they walk away. If I'm in restaurant with my family and I'm about to put a Yorkshire pudding in my mouth, what the hell do you expect? Some people just don't get it.

Me and the wife and kids were going to Alton Towers a few weeks ago and so before we went I decided to take action. We'd been to West Midlands Safari Park a few months before that and while we were sitting having a drink I must have been asked for a photo about twenty times. Given my size, I might not be the most famous man in the world but I'm definitely one of the most conspicuous. When you see me coming it must be like Mr Stay Puft from *Ghostbusters*. Either that or a barrage balloon. I don't stand a chance.

When I say I took action before we went to Alton Towers, what I mean is that I asked my mum if I could borrow her beanie hat. She looked at me as if I was mad and when I attempted to put it on it was like trying to cover the moon with a tablecloth. In the end I wore a hoodie and some sunglasses, but it made no difference whatsoever. Sure enough, within about ten minutes of being there I was mobbed and so we ended up coming home. That's obviously not ideal but what can you do? If I'd wanted to have a quiet life I should have become a librarian.

I think the most embarrassing situation I've ever been in, certainly with regards to being recognised, happened at an Expo I attended a few years ago. I won't say where or when it was for the sake of the person involved, but I'm telling you now it was a damn close shave and involved an incredible piece of acting.

I'd been asked to do a photoshoot at this Expo that involved me picking up some girls and balancing them on my shoulder. It's something I get asked to do a lot, not surprisingly, and a couple of weeks ago I even had the Lord Mayor of Stoke on my shoulders. Anyway, just after I'd finished this photoshoot a couple of girls came up to me and asked me if I could do the same with them. Their boyfriends were already poised with cameras and so I thought, *Yeah, why the hell not?* They only weighed about eight stone wet through and so I'd hardly notice they were there. Thirty seconds later another two girls came up and asked the same, so I obliged. I did feel a bit like a fucking fairground ride by this point but hey ho, it's nice to give something back. Once the two girls were safely on the ground I shouted, 'Who's next?' but before I could stand up straight again I managed to catch a glimpse of the lower half of the person next in the queue. And thank fuck I did. She was standing with her back to me and as well as having calves the size of rugby balls, she had thighs like rubber dinghies and an arse that should really have had its own time zone. Quick as a flash I grabbed my back and started grimacing.

'Oh fuck,' I cried. 'My back!'

As I pretended to try to straighten myself without success, this girl and her boyfriend approached me and asked me if I was OK.

'I was in a competition a few days ago,' I lied. 'And I'm still a bit sore. I'll be OK. No more lifting gorgeous women, though. Sorry, love.'

The poor girl looked absolutely gutted but what could I do? It wasn't her weight that was the problem. It was getting it from the ground onto my shoulders, and then keeping it there. I'm a strongman, not a fucking pendulum ride!

Funnily enough, it was at this Expo that I entered my first, and last, nail-hammering competition, which resulted in me experiencing something that, hitherto, had been alien to me: humiliation. Throughout my years in strongman – and in swimming – I'd had everything thrown at me: I'd been sent home, reprimanded, shouted at, disqualified, fined, docked points and even beaten on one or two occasions. But never humiliated. Then, at this Expo, somebody thought that because I was big and strong I'd be ideal as a nail hammerer. And they were right, in the first instance. The prize for winning this competition was two tickets to the British Moto GP at Silverstone as well as qualification to the final of the British Nail-Hammering Championship. Who knew there was such a thing? (I certainly didn't.) And first prize for winning that was a brand-new motorbike worth a cool £10,000. Dad was with me at this Expo and I remember saying to him, ''Ere. I'm going to have that fucking bike. Watch this.'

All you had to do was hammer a ten-inch nail into a piece of hardwood and whoever did it the quickest, won. Dad had already had a go and to be fair to him he was one of the fastest yet. About fifteen seconds, if memory serves. I think I was one of the last people to attempt it and I remember picking up the nail, resting it on the block, and within three hits it was flush with the wood. BANG, BANG, BANG! Job done. After soaking up the applause, I looked at Dad, winked, and said, rather presumptuously, 'Dad, how do you fancy going to Silverstone to pick up my new bike?' Dad's a big motorbike man and I knew he'd be up for going to the GP. 'OK, son,' he said. 'I'll tag along.'

About a month later Dad and I were on our way to Silverstone for the Grand Prix weekend and the competition. I'd already decided what I was going to do with the bike: sell it, and pocket the cash. What I was going to do with the cash I still hadn't decided, but I'd already told Alex it was coming in. 'Ten big ones, honey,' I'd said to her. 'And all for knocking in a fucking nail.'

When Dad and I got to where they were having the competition there was an actual Moto GP bike on display in the room and because everyone was taking photographs of me I decided to pick up the bike and pose with it. You should have seen the looks on the organisers' faces. What a picture! As I was hoisting it aloft, Dad sidled up to me and whispered, 'That bike's worth a quarter of a million pounds. For fuck's sake, don't drop it!'

There were ten people in the final of this British Nail Hammering Championship and I was the biggest by half a foot and at least ten stone. It was in the bag.

First up was a lad from North Yorkshire. I forget his name (let's call him Jim Smith), but I'll never forget his occupation.

'First up,' said the man with the mic, 'is Mr Jim Smith from North Yorkshire. Occupation: farrier.'

I looked at Dad and said, 'What the fuck's a farrier, Dad?'

For some reason he looked worried. 'Somebody who knocks in nails for a living, son,' he said.

'Yeah, but he's only about five foot nine inches. Nothing to worry about.'

Unbeknownst to me, the hardwood had been replaced by a kind of laminate block, which was about ten times harder, and as opposed to whacking the nail as hard as he could, this bloke was tapping it very quickly. It was going in, but only slowly.

'Fuck me, Dad,' I said. 'He's taking forever. Why doesn't he just whack it?'

Dad didn't say a word and just stood there with his arms folded.

'Next up,' said the man with the mic, 'is Mr Mike Green from Dorset. Occupation: farrier.'

Chapter 29

Yet again, this bloke was only knee high to a grasshopper.

'I'm a bit worried about this,' said Dad.

'Don't be,' I replied. 'Have you seen how fast they are? I'll piss it.'

As it turned out, the first four contestants were all farriers and as well as their styles being identical, their times were all similar too. Even so, I was still confident that power would prevail and when I walked up to the block and picked up my nail I was as confident as I'd ever been. *Watch this*, I said to myself.

As I tried to rest the nail on the block it started sliding around. *Strange,* I thought. *Seems a bit hard to me.* At the Expo I'd managed to make a tiny hole with the nail that had kept it in place. This time though, it was a lot more difficult.

'Ready?' said the time keeper. 'Three, two, one, GO!'

I lifted up the hammer, and with all the power I could muster I brought it down on top of the nail. 'BANG!'

Instead of penetrating the block, the nail stayed exactly where it was and just bent slightly. 'Bollocks!' I said. I picked up another nail and tried again but this time it flew off the table. *What the hell's going on?* I thought. *This stuff's like steel!*

Anyway, to cut a pitifully long story short I didn't win the motorbike and the farriers, one of whom did win it, obviously knew exactly what they were doing. Good for them.

As opposed to hanging around for the Grand Prix, which was the following day, I called Mum straight after the competition and told her that she could come and take my place. I was just appalled with myself.

Getting back to fame briefly, the thing that really pisses me off, although it doesn't happen any more, is when people come to my house. I have a zero-tolerance policy when it comes to this sort of thing and the last person who tried it got a fucking battering. It was in 2014 and we were sitting at home having a quiet evening when somebody did a knock and run. Although I didn't get out in time to catch them, I'd had CCTV installed and so went to have a look. It was actually a gang of local teenagers who I recognised, but because they all had hoodies on, I couldn't pinpoint who did it. Anyway, I knew full well that they all hung out in the park and so I climbed into my car and drove up there.

As expected, every single one of the little bastards was there and when they saw me walking towards them they panicked. Fortunately, I didn't have to run as there was only one way out and so once I was in position I gave them the full SP. 'Right then, fuckers,' I began. 'Which one of you bastards knocked on my door and ran off?' Obviously, nobody said a word and everyone just shrugged their shoulders. 'I'll tell you what,' I said. 'If you don't tell me who did it I'm going to smack every single one of you. Did you get that? You will all leave here with a black eye.' There was probably about twelve of them in total and the moment I'd finished talking they all pointed to this one kid. 'Right then, you,' I said, before picking him up by the scruff of the neck. 'You're coming with me.'

Believe it or not I can be quite menacing when I want to be and by the time I'd got this kid into my car he was absolutely cacking himself. In fact, he was actually whimpering.

'All I'm going to do,' I said to him, 'is take you back to my house and you're going to apologise to my wife, and if you don't, I'm going to strangle you.'

The apology Alex received was sincere (although the delivery was a bit stuttery) and when he finally finished talking I kicked him up the arse and sent him on his way.

You see, to me, stuff like that is crossing the line, both literally and metaphorically. My wife and kids live in that house and if you start doing things like that there's a chance you might scare them or, worse still, put them in danger. I might not be the greatest dad or husband on the planet but I'll stop at nothing to make sure they're safe.

Anyway, let's get back to the story. Becoming famous was (generally) a nice side-effect of my work as a professional strongman, but the real business was to keep hauling myself further up the ladder to the top ...

CHAPTER 30

Captured on Camera

Four weeks after returning home from Melbourne I was back on a plane to Malaysia for the 2015 World's Strongest Man. Even though I'd only been pro for a few months it had already started paying dividends and I was confident that, if I hadn't caught the top three, I'd at least have made ground on them. In terms of a result, anything better than sixth would do, but because of the progress I'd made I was confident of finishing at least fourth.

Without wanting to sound like a bighead, qualifying was a piece of piss and by the time the final arrived I was bigger and stronger than I'd ever been. The problem was, so were Brian, Thor and Žydrūnas. Actually, at almost forty years of age, Žydrūnas Savickas was probably just a fraction past his best at this point. Even so, he was still the most experienced strongman there and only a fool would have written him off.

The competition finished with Brian first on fifty-three points, Žydrūnas second on forty-nine and a half (I told you!), Thor third on forty-nine, and me fourth on forty-five and a half. Brian Shaw was on imperious form that year and although I didn't win an event outright, I did manage to whip Thor's ass on the atlas stones, which not many people can claim to have done. As this was the finale of the competition, I was determined to do well and I only just got beaten by Brian on time.

What gave me the most amount of satisfaction that year was the knowledge that I was now knocking on the door of the top three and everything I'd prophesised prior to becoming a professional was starting to come true.

The only thing that wasn't working out was my home life. I'd had this notion that, once I'd gone full time, I'd be able to devote more time to my family. Fat chance! As well as obviously spending more time in the gym, I was also spending more time recovering – which could be anything from having physio to hot and cold treatments – and that's something that takes up an awful lot of time. Then you have eating. I was now well on my way to being thirty stone and that takes time – and preparation. So, if I wasn't eating or sleeping, I was training, and if I wasn't training, I was either recovering or researching. Somewhere in between all that I had to try and fit in my sponsor commitments, not to mention the media, so actually, I was probably spending less time with the family than I had when I was a truck mechanic. The only difference was that we had a plan now, something to aim for, and that – for the time being, at least – was papering over the cracks.

The last major strongman event of 2015 was Europe's Strongest Man, which, as always, kicked off with the

World Deadlift Championships. Unfortunately, I ended up sustaining an injury during the main event but managed to win the World Deadlift Championships in style. By now, I was starting to pull away from the crowd at deadlift and nobody in the world could come anywhere near me. I knew it, and so did they. I was already the best there had ever been.

In the end, I broke my own world record by a kilogram. Oh, and I did it as a speed rep. You watch any other strongman lift anything over 430kg (948 lb) and the majority will be as slow as an eight-day clock and close to fucking dying. Not me. This is what I live for.

Anyway, just to prove how fucking fantastic I was, here are the results from the World Deadlift Championships that year:

1. Eddie Hall 463kg/1020 lb: New World Record
2. Hafthor Björnsson 450kg/992 lb
3. Jerry Prichett and Rauno Heinla 435kg/959 lb
4. Andy Bolton 420kg/925 lb
5. Terry Hollands, Krzystophe Radzikowski, Mark Felix, Dainis Zageris, Matjaz Belsak, 400kg/881 lb
6. Dimitar Savitinov 360kg/793 lb

That wasn't the only good thing that came out of this year either. You may have noticed but throughout the book I keep on referring to 'the documentary'. For those of you who aren't aware, it's called *Eddie – Strongman*, it's absolutely fucking amazing, it's on Netflix and on DVD, and it was released towards the end of 2015.

The brainchild behind the documentary, Matt Bell, isn't a child, but he definitely has a brain, as when he decided a few years ago that he wanted to make a documentary about a strongman, he chose me. As I said, the man's not daft.

Matt had been a presenter on *UK's Strongest Man* for a couple of years but really he was a film maker and when he first approached me back in 2012 I was surprised, but I was definitely interested. I obviously wasn't sure if anything would come of it – such is the world of film-making – but it was definitely worth a punt. First and foremost, I trusted Matt and I liked him. I was also flattered; as you know, I like having my feathers stroked.

The first thing we had to sort out was the money, or rather Matt did. We generated the majority of it via crowd-funding but Matt also put a lot of his own money in and we managed to get one or two sponsors. When filming began at the start of 2013 I was surprised by how full on it was. There were only usually one or two people present – Matt and one other – but they were there all the frigging time and after a week or so I remember thinking, *What the fucking hell have I done?* When somebody says, 'We'll be following you all the time,' you don't take them literally. Or at least I didn't. Matt had gone to great lengths to explain everything, though, so it was my own fault. I was just going to have to get used to it.

The premiere was as posh as fuck and took place at the Mayfair Hotel in London on 19 December 2015. There's a private cinema there that holds about 200 people and after the screening we did a Q&A on stage before getting absolutely trollied. It was a hell of a night, and, all credit to Mr Bell, it's one hell of a film. Since then it's been picked up by Netflix and has been on there ever since. In fact, it even trended on Netflix for several months so God knows how many people have seen it. There is talk of there being a sequel to the documentary, but I can't say any more at the moment. Don't bet against it happening.

Talking of bets. I'm just about to have one on myself.

CHAPTER 31

Preparing to Lift Half a Tonne

The idea to attempt a half-tonne deadlift first came about directly after the 2015 World Deadlift Championships (which was the support event for Europe's Strongest Man) where I'd broken the world record by pulling 463kg (1,020 lb). I'm pretty sure this is on camera somewhere but I remember saying to Colin Bryce after the show that if he could find a backer who'd be willing to put up the cash, I would pull half a tonne at next year's event. Now, I know for a fact that Colin didn't think I could pull 500kg (1,102 lb) at the time (nobody in the world did apart from me), but he obviously thought it would make a good spectacle and so without pissing around he found a backer and told me we were on.

At the time, such a lift was considered to be impossible and I remember reading discussions on strength forums entitled, 'Will we ever see a 1,100-lb deadlift?' Every single person who replied to that initial question said no, it would never happen, and thinking about it sensibly, you can understand why.

Since time immemorial, if somebody had attempted to break the world deadlift record they'd probably go up by 1kg (2.2 lb), which is what the likes of Benni and I had been doing for a couple of years. It wasn't something that happened every day, and because not all attempts were successful it was obviously a very gradual progression. Going up by a massive 37kg (82 lb), or about 8 per cent, was beyond ridiculous but what sealed the deal and made everyone assume it was impossible wasn't the increase, it was the weight itself. Half a tonne is the equivalent of a very heavy racehorse and, to the vast majority of sane human beings, that was beyond the possibilities of man.

It was these pundits' certainty – their unequivocalness – that first caught my imagination. The more people told me that a half-tonne deadlift couldn't be done, the more I told myself it could.

As a challenge this ticked so many boxes for me. First, but not foremost, it had a good lump of cash attached to it and as a professional strongman that was music to my ears. Secondly, I'd be doing something that nobody had ever done before in the history of the world and that in itself floated my boat big-time. Do you know that since time began, over 110 billion people have walked the Earth? If I did manage to lift half a tonne off the ground I'd be making history, and it didn't matter how many people either matched it or bettered me in the future, I'd always be the first. That's the difference between something like this and winning World's Strongest Man. Winning that title means you follow in the footsteps of some amazing athletes and it means you'll always be part of what is a very special club. That's just it, though, you're part of a club. One of many. Following in other people's footsteps doesn't make you a history maker. The last tick-box, and by far the biggest, was that it provided me with the ultimate motivation – that nobody in the world (that I was aware of) thought it was possible. That really is my lifeblood.

When I eventually went public with my intentions, the reactions from people were perfect: a mixture of negativity and incredulity. I knew I could find encouragement if I needed it (and I was sure I'd be needing some on the night), but for the time being I was quite happy feeding off all the pisstakers and naysayers. Their negativity fuelled my positivity and if it hadn't been for so many people doubting me I don't think I'd have been arsed. Seriously. If everyone had turned around to me and said, 'Do you know what, Ed, I reckon you're going to pull that half a tonne,' I'd never have attempted it. Proving myself right is fantastic, but proving others wrong is even better.

The icing on the cake was seeing Brian Shaw and Žydrūnas Savickas, two of the strongest men who've ever lived, both come out and say that it couldn't be done. They didn't take the piss or anything, they were just giving their honest beliefs. I remember Brian saying that he simply thought it wasn't possible, whereas Žydrūnas thought it could only end in injury. Maybe he was right?

The only distractions I'd had leading up to the lift, apart from a few personal appearances, had been Britain's Strongest

Man, so I'd been able to remain pretty focused. I'd worked out that in order for me to support 500kg I would have to weigh at least 185kg (408 lb). That meant putting on over 15kg (33 lb) in the final six months. I did it, just, but a lot of that went on in the final few weeks. From the second I woke up until the moment I went to bed I would either have food in my mouth, in my hand, or within reaching distance. There was no science behind the 185kg, by the way, it was just an educated guess. I needed something to work towards, and 35 per cent of the weight I was lifting seemed about right.

That's one of the mad things about my sport; we don't have any coaches or advisors. Given what we do in the gym and at competitions that's absolutely ridiculous. I was looking at the event list for World's Strongest Man the other day and I thought to myself, *In a few weeks*' time I'm going to be on the other side of the world doing Viking presses, tyre flips, truck pulls and atlas stones at the biggest strength event on the planet yet I have never been coached in any one of these events. Now you can look at that in one of two ways: you can either you shake your head and think, *That's a disgrace! Why doesn't the sport do more?* Or you can see it as an opportunity and work out how you can change things for the better. Welcome to the Eddie Hall school of strongman! It could happen.

That's another paradox. Successful strongmen, on the whole, are bright guys, and the reason I know that is because we're left to our own devices so we have to figure it out for ourselves if we want to do well. It doesn't matter how much natural talent you have, if you can't work out how to train properly, refine your technique and work out what food to eat, you're going to get left behind. It's not just survival of the fittest, it's survival of the sharpest.

Let me give you a quick example of exactly how this culture of self-sufficiency has worked for me. About a year ago I was in Sweden doing a guest appearance at an expo and about half way through I was told by the organisers that in ten minutes' time I'd be required to do a demonstration deadlift of 400kg (881 lb). It wasn't anybody's fault but unfortunately this hadn't been communicated to me so I told them that I wasn't ready.

'Don't worry, Eddie,' they said. 'We'll get you ready.'

About two minutes later this bloke walks in carrying what looked like an enormous car buffer. 'What the hell's that?' I asked him.

'Watch this,' he said, and before I could say another word he started working my back and warming me up with this huge car buffer.

'How's that?' he asked.

'Fucking unbelievable,' I replied. 'Better than any warm up I could ever do.'

It was astonishing. Five minutes later I went out into the hall, pulled the 400kg and I was fine. Job done. The moment I got back home I went straight out and bought one of these things and it's now become an important part of my warm-up routine. If I'd been surrounded by coaches and the like I would never have discovered that machine and the fact that I did makes me appreciate my autonomy even more.

Something else that's made a big difference to me lately, although this is actually quite specialist, is a mouth guard. The idea, in layman's terms, is that if your jaw's moving about a lot then your body follows suit. Keep your jaw fixed, however, and you will remain far more stable and balanced. Believe me it works and is worth at least a couple of extra reps.

Something that you'll all have seen strongmen use over the years are smelling salts. Even though we know what's coming they work purely via the element of surprise. Honestly, taking a good sniff of that stuff is like being slapped in the face and the reason strongmen pull so many ridiculous faces when we take a sniff of smelling salts is because it makes us want to kill somebody! Once you've had some of that you can lift pretty much anything. Or at least you feel like you can.

Although deadlift was already part of my training routine, I started refining and modernising the sessions from the moment the attempt was confirmed, which was about a year before. Each week I'd alternate between heavy lifting and speed, and then, at the end of every quarter, I'd go for a new personal best. Thursdays were deadlift day and so as soon as I arrived at the gym I'd go straight to the deadlift platform. To warm up for deadlift I always do what's called a 'pyramid up' – one plate ten reps, two plates eight reps, etc. – and then I stretch. I cannot emphasise enough the importance of stretching, regardless of what you do in the gym. Fail to do it properly and as well as never realising your full potential you're bound to do yourself an injury. A lot of people just can't be arsed and that's madness. Take my word for it, when it comes to training it's as essential as the exercise itself.

All the way through this session I would be eating bananas and drinking cranberry juice. Fast-acting sugars, basically. Once the heavy lifting started I would then eat lumps of steak between each lift. This provided me with natural proteins, natural BCAAs and natural fats. As far as I know I'm the only person who does this but I'd definitely recommend it. It obviously costs a bit but it's worth the investment.

Before I went professional I could only manage one heavy-lifting session every two weeks as that was the time it took my body to recover. A deadlift, remember, is the only exercise that uses every part of your body, so it makes sense. Everything kills! After going pro, I discovered things like hot and cold treatments and massage. Each one reduced my recovery time, so the more I added to the programme, the quicker I could start lifting again. Once again there's a cost attached to it but I don't view that as a barrier, I view it as a motivation. If it's the right thing to do you can always find a way.

Despite all the massages and ice baths etc., I was in constant pain, especially during the last few weeks before the record attempt. Getting out of bed to eat in the morning was absolutely excruciating and it took me every minute of the time I had between getting up and going to the gym to prepare myself for the next session. Even at home I had to try to block myself off, so despite living with my family physically, we had to be separated emotionally. I know that's not ideal, especially when you have small children, but that's the way it had to be. Mentally, I was in a very, very dark place leading up to the lift, so even if I had been able to communicate with my family I would probably either have screamed at them or burst out crying. I'm not sure if it was a depression, exactly. It was just somewhere I had to go. Strangely enough, that actually formed part of my motivation, as I knew it would only last until the lift. Do the job right and it would evaporate immediately. Fail, and it might stay.

Not one aspect of this practice is healthy, of course, but it's what I had to do. Alex and I have been through hell over the last seven years – or rather, I've put her through hell – but what keeps us together is the fact that she knows I'm doing it all for us. Completing the lift would go some way to offering us financial security but I have to admit that I hadn't envisaged it being quite so intense. Alex and I have been on the verge of splitting up several times and the vast majority of women would probably have walked out long ago. It certainly hasn't been easy. It rarely is with me.

About two weeks prior to the lift I started having heart palpitations. This was obviously down to the pressure, but the more I had the palpitations the more I thought something was wrong and so it became self-perpetuating. It was all my own fault. I'd created so much hype within the strength community that, should I not manage the lift, I'd be a complete laughing stock. So despite being in perfect shape (apart from the heart!), I now had an element of doubt. Paradoxically, this was probably as essential to my final preparations as confidence itself. Why? Because with over-confidence comes complacency and in order to prevent complacency from creeping in you have to maintain self-awareness. Believe me, a seed or two of doubt can do wonders for your self-awareness. The perspective isn't always balanced, but at least you're looking in the right direction.

I'd made an awful lot of claims in my time but, God willing, I'd always managed to back them up. This one was different, though, as basically I was attempting to separate myself from every other strongman who had ever lived. I was trying to create my own exclusive club. One that, regardless of which way it went, would only ever have one member: the first man to lift half a tonne – or, the first man to fail to lift half a tonne. One was quite desirable; the other, not so much.

Now I had only one day to go before the attempt. The next day would be the day I went down in history, or died trying.

CHAPTER 32

The Day of the Dead(lift)

The day before the event I drove up to Leeds in silence. I often do that as it helps me to focus and plan, and on this occasion there was only one thing to focus on but a lot to plan. For a start, I was beginning to worry whether I'd be able to sleep that night and so somewhere on the M1 I started to devise a strategy. Actually, it was more a concoction really and involved 1000mg of tramadol (the maximum dose is usually 500mg) and about three shots of whisky. Sometimes a bit of insomnia can keep you sharp but this was different. Had I not taken anything I know for a fact that I wouldn't have slept a wink and bearing in mind what I was attempting that would have spelled disaster. Fortunately, the whisky and the tramadol worked a treat and when I woke up the following morning I felt like a new man. I started shitting myself again soon after, but the first five minutes or so were great!

Incidentally, the previous day I'd gone out into Leeds and bought myself twenty litres of Lucozade, as you do, and by the time I went to bed that night, every single bottle was empty. I drink something similar prior to every event and for a time afterwards my entire body glistens and swells up. What's even more amazing, on that occasion, is that despite consuming such a vast amount of liquid I didn't go to the toilet once. Every drop was absorbed and used.

The first thing I did that morning was have a protein shake. Actually, it's the first thing I do every morning! Then, after napping for another hour I went out and had the biggest, fattiest fried breakfast you have ever seen in your life. I think I had six or seven sausages, five big rashers of bacon, four eggs, loads of mushrooms, four hash browns, some tomatoes and baked beans. Then, at about 10 a.m., I went out again and had a huge bowl of porridge. It was more a bucket really. After stretching off I went back to bed and had a couple of hours' kip. I do always sleep, by the way, when I go back to bed. I don't just sit there and watch TV. It's an essential part of my recovery.

For lunch, I went to an all-you-can-eat meat restaurant and asked the chef to cook me off any fat he had from either pork or gammon. Nice image, isn't it? Just thinking about it makes me want to puke, but at 9 calories per gram it was worth about 4,000 calories. It looked, tasted and smelt absolutely rank and the chef must have thought I had some kind of weird fetish. I tried to explain what I wanted it for but as I was talking he just walked slowly backwards.

By this time, Rich, my physio had arrived, so, after spending another hour in bed and then eating some flapjacks, I got up and had a nice long physio session before heading off to the arena. I always like to arrive at these places at least half an hour before everyone else as it gives me the chance to acclimatise. Something else I do which nobody else does is spend some time in the arena while it's empty. Then, when people start arriving, I periodically wander out there again. This prevents me from becoming either nervous or overcome by the amount of people present and, as well as helping me get used to the noise, it allows me to utilise the energy the crowd can generate. I've seen dozens of athletes walk out in front of a full arena and it scares them half to death. Just for a moment they forget what they're actually there for and by the time they've pulled themselves together they've lost a lot of impetus.

Something else I have to watch out for are changes in temperature. Because of the amount of isotonic liquids I drink I'm boiling hot before a competition and am like a massive ball of energy. It's important that I maintain that heat and keep all the energy in, so sharp changes in temperature, especially lower temperatures, are a definite no-no.

With regards to contact, I hardly speak to a soul in the lead-up to a lift or a competition. In fact, on this particular occasion I decided to put my earphones in. The music I always listen to is Eminem, which takes me back to my very early high school days. That was a time when I didn't give a shit about anything, so as well as keeping me focused it helps level me out emotionally. A few happy memories are just what you need sometimes.

If anyone comes to talk to me prior to an event I always shake my head and look away but on this occasion, apart from the people on my team, no one came anywhere near me. There was one occasion when somebody did disturb me and unfortunately they bore the full brunt of my anger. It happened in the gym, just before I was due to attempt a 400kg (881 lb) squat. As usual, I'd been stomping up and down like a dinosaur psyching myself up. Then the last thing I did before attempting the squat was look in the mirror, have a few words with myself and sniff some smelling salts. As I'm standing there telling myself how fucking strong I am, this kid walked up and tapped me on the back. Because I was so massively revved up I just ignored him but the stupid prat tried again. This time I'm afraid I just lost it and backhanded him. I didn't look, I just smacked him in the face. After that he must have gone scampering off and I did my lift. I said to my training partner Luke afterwards, 'Who the fuck was that tapping me on the shoulder?'

'No idea,' he said. 'But you proper smacked him in the face.'

I obviously felt pretty bad about it afterwards but at the end of the day I was focused and ready to lift. If you're daft enough to tap me on the shoulder when I'm in the zone, for fuck's sake don't do it a second time!

One thing I noticed as I was warming up at the arena was that all eyes were on me. Every single athlete and crew member was just staring at me. There was also silence, which there never usually is. At last, I think some doubt was creeping in. Not for me, but for them. If they thought I hadn't stood a chance they'd have been carrying on as usual, but backstage at the Leeds Arena at 7 p.m. on Saturday 9 July 2016 you could have heard a fucking pin drop.

The three athletes who were competing at the World Deadlift Championship were me, Benni Magnússon and Jerry Pritchett, and all three of us had agreed to go for the 500kg (1,102 lb). The other athletes present were obviously there for Europe's Strongest Man but to be honest there seemed to be more interest in the lift. This was history, remember.

As the three of us were doing a few warm-up lifts, I remember thinking, *Have either of these two got it in them to lift 500kg?* Benni seemed to be getting very worked up prior to lifting 300kg (661 lb). He was literally shaking with anger. It was only a warm-up though, so what was the point in that? He also lifted it very, very quickly, so as opposed to warming up, what he was actually doing was expending some of his energy and adrenalin.

A few minutes later, while he was still pumped up, Benni came up to me and as well as telling me I wouldn't lift the 500kg, he also said he'd lift more than me that day. Even though we were rivals, Benni and I had trained together once or twice and generally we got on very well. There was a difference between us, though, and that difference was exemplified right there and then. 'Do you know what I see in your eyes, Benni?' I said to him. 'I see me lifting 500kg.' The moment I said that, Benni's head lowered and his body language completely changed. I knew he wouldn't get anywhere near me, and certainly nowhere near 500kg. The thing is, so did he. I didn't want to head-fuck Benni but it had to be done. It was just me and the bar now.

When it came to the running order I asked to be first out and for two simple reasons. First and foremost, I wanted to be the first man to lift 500kg. I was adamant that neither Benni nor Jerry (ice cream, anyone?) were up to it but I still wanted an insurance policy. And secondly, I didn't want to see anyone else fail. Normally that might have spurred me on but Žydrūnas Savickas had been right when he said there was a high chance of injury and the last thing I wanted to see was somebody tearing a hamstring off. That would have put me off completely.

The night before at the athletes meeting, Benni and I had almost come to blows over who would pull first. It was proper handbags! I'd said to the promoters that I wanted to go first and straightaway Benni said that he did. 'Why the fuck should you go first?' I said. 'The 500kg was my idea and at the end of the day I'm the one who's got the best chance of lifting it.' Naturally, Benni didn't quite agree with me and for the next thirty minutes or so we carried on arguing. 'Let's toss a coin,' suggested one of the promoters. 'Fuck your coin,' I said. 'I'm going first and that's that.' In the end I think I managed to wear Benni down because after what must have been about forty-five minutes he held his hands up and said, 'If it means that much to you, go first!' I think I must have bored him into submission.

Now at last we were almost ready to go. Backstage, Benni and Jerry lifted 380kg (838 lb) and 400kg (881 lb) to warm up (I opted out). The first lift we needed to do onstage was 420kg (925 lb). I walked out into the spotlights, Colin Bryce introduced me to the crowd and the moment he said my name the entire place just erupted. It was a real hairs-on-the-back-of-your-neck moment.

About ten seconds later, I'd pulled the 420kg and after winking at the camera I walked off stage thinking, *That didn't take long*. It was a fucking speed rep! The next lift was 440kg (970 lb), which I decided to skip, and after that it was going to be 465kg (1,025 lb), which would be a new world record. Once again, I walked onstage to thunderous applause and to show my appreciation I pulled it as a speed rep again. Seriously, you watch it back on YouTube. Blink and you'll miss it. After me it was Jerry and Benni's turn, and fair play to them, they pulled it too. They didn't manage to speed rep it, but they were good lifts.

By this point I knew for a fact that I was going to pull 500kg and the only things worrying me now were Benni and Jerry. The deal was that, regardless of who went first, if more than one person pulled it we'd have to share the record and that was obviously only fair. Was there a chance they might lift it too? Christ, I hoped not. I wanted to keep all the glory for myself and as awful as it might sound I remember willing them to fail.

Apart from the ice cream brothers preying on my mind, in the minutes leading up to the lift everything was perfect. My team especially were textbook and I couldn't have wished to have had better people around me. They were Rich, my physio; Luke, my training partner; Rob Frampton, the strongman; and Andy Parker, who owns my gym. All four of these guys are friends of mine but as importantly, with regards to the situation, they're the most positive people you could ever meet, especially Rob Frampton. After he'd finished talking to me I could have walked on fucking water. That man can seriously empower people.

While Rob was massaging my ego and putting chalk on my hands, I had Rich massaging my legs, Andy putting my belt on and Luke sorting out my mouth guard. All this had been planned beforehand, by the way. The idea being that I wouldn't have to think about anything other than the lift. I couldn't wait to get out there now.

At about 7.45 p.m. a crew member came into my room to ask me politely if there was anything I needed. As per my usual practice, I told him in no uncertain terms to fuck off. The people at Giants Live know what I'm like at events and it was nothing personal. In fact, I think they expect it now. The last thing to go on was my T-shirt with my sponsors on. Now I was ready.

'We've still got a few minutes,' said Rob. 'I'll tell you what. Let's go for a walk.'

To get a bit of peace and quiet we all decamped to a disabled toilet where Rob carried on speaking the gospel. I needed to be in a confined space with positive people and this was our only option. Not very glamorous I know, but it's who you're with that's important, not where you are. As Rob spoke I stared at myself in the mirror. Normally when I'm trying to psych myself up I'll start thinking about very dark things. Things that make me angry. The psychology behind this is quite obvious as the angrier I become, the more adrenalin I have running through my veins. Once I'm incandescent with rage, I'll stare at myself and say, 'Now.' That's all. 'Now.' Less is definitely more in these situations.

By the time our impromptu motivational get-together had come to an end I was on the brink of spontaneously combusting. Without any further ado, I turned around, kicked open the door and we made our way to the stage.

Once we were stage-side, the lads started checking everything and making sure I was happy. I was. I was good to go. The crowd had been absolutely fantastic all night but as I walked out to the bar they seemed to go quiet all of a sudden. Perhaps they were nervous?

'Come on, you buggers!' I remember shouting, and then I gestured. 'Give us a hand!'

Fortunately their response was both loud and immediate but as I was standing there taking it all in I started to have what some people might call an out-of-body experience. It was bizarre, but all I could see for about five seconds was me, in position, locking out the lift. I was about fifty yards away looking down at the stage, and all I saw was me. It was self-belief TV.

Once the vision of me had gone and I was back in the arena I locked onto the bar, doing up my straps and checking my breathing. Then I got my feet and shoulders in line. *Right then, Eddie*, I thought. *Time to go*. I took a big breath and then another. The moment that second breath was completely in I tensed up momentarily, let it out, and then went to take what would have to be the biggest breath of my entire life. I don't know how many cubic centimetres of air I took into my lungs but it was enough to blow up a bouncy castle. Once that breath was held I started pulling the bar in towards my shins. My eyes were closed now and I couldn't hear a thing. As the bar slammed against my shins I leaned back, put all the weight into my arse and as I rolled forward I remember thinking to myself, *For fuck's sake Eddie, try and make it look easy!* How ridiculous is that? Here I am, about to try and lift half a tonne, and all I'm bothered about is how it looks!

From the moment I took the strain I knew I had enough power to nail it. My entire body had been quite loose until then but the moment I started to lift, all the energy came together and it just went BOOM! You can actually see the bar shudder at this point and as it's coming up I'm standing there thinking, *I've got this. I've fucking got it!* Internally I was laughing my arse off. Not because I was happy, although I was. Oh no. This was an evil laugh! A laugh that signified my revenge. As I locked out the lift I remember shouting, 'Fuck you!' which was directed at every single person who'd said it couldn't be done. It could be done, but only by one man.

The next thing I remember is waking up looking at a massive pool of blood. My blood, apparently. There must have been about a litre of it, but as well as it streaming out of my nose it was also coming out of my ears and even my eyes. My beard was drenched in it.

As the medics came in and started taking my belt and the straps off, my body started convulsing. I was also going in and out of consciousness at this point so for the first twenty seconds or so I had no control over my body. The first voice I remember hearing was one of the medics saying, 'You've got to get up, Ed. You've got to get up and let people know you're OK.' As he was saying this two other medics were busy wiping blood out of my eyes and ears.

Once I was fully conscious again I decided I'd had enough of this attention and so once they'd finished cleaning me up I started telling them all to fuck off. This took everyone by surprise and they scattered like school children. It was such an emotional moment though and the more conscious I became of my surroundings the more I realised what I'd just achieved. From that moment on it was just a groundswell of emotions. A culmination of spending twelve months in hell. I remember looking at the 10,000 people in front of me and it was unbelievable. People were either crying, cheering or just standing there with their mouths open. Either way, what I think we were experiencing was a variation of exactly the same thing: a mixture of extreme joy and shock.

Colin Bryce, who is never normally short of a few words, was just standing there looking at me and shaking his head. Colin Bryce has almost as much faith in my abilities as I do and by the day of the competition I reckon he was one of the few people who thought I could do it. He always told me I could, and I love him for that, but if truth be known there was only one person in the world who really believed I could pull that lift a year ago and he'd just lost a litre or so of blood in the process. The point at which that changed was when I pulled 465kg as a speed rep and once that happened you could feel the atmosphere change in the arena. Before that it had been one of enthusiasm. Everyone had been enjoying themselves and who knows, they might even see a world record. But the moment I pulled that lift everything flipped and all that enthusiasm changed to expectation. Now they were expecting not just a world record, but *the* world record. That memory of me standing there looking at the audience's faces is one of the most vivid I have and it will stay with me for the rest of my life.

One of the first people to congratulate me after the lift was Benni. Both he and Jerry attempted the lift after me as arranged, and although Benni had managed to get it off the ground it was only by a few inches. Poor Jerry ended up pulling a hamstring during his attempt and so in some ways Žydrūnas had been proved right.

'I knew you were going to pull it,' Benni said to me. 'I just didn't realise you were going to pull it so fast, you fucking freak!'

Bearing in mind we'd been adversaries for a couple of years that was a really sweet thing to do and if I'd had the energy

I'd have given him a big hug. As it was, I was well and truly F.U.C.K.E.D. and had hit a rather large wall. My skin was now so pale it seemed almost transparent and even twenty minutes after the lift my heart rate was still just over 160. That's nothing, though. Ever since he arrived, the doctor, who said I shouldn't have been alive, had been trying to take my blood pressure but according to him it was so high it was off the charts. He estimated that twenty minutes after the lift it was about 300 over 180, which is beyond dangerous. That's the reason I'd started bleeding out of so many orifices. 'All that blood has got to go somewhere, Eddie,' the doctor had said. 'If it hadn't come out of your nose, your eyes and your ears, your heart would probably have exploded.' That made me feel miles better!

Actually, I was starting to feel a lot worse again and despite them feeding me lots of sugars and carbs I was back to being in and out of consciousness. This was different, though, almost as if I was stoned, and as well as me thinking I had massive hands everyone around me seemed to have two heads. It was all very trippy!

About two hours later I was just about able to stand up, but only just. Medically, it had been the scariest two hours of my life and was my body's way of telling me I'd had a very narrow escape. The only thing I can compare it to was the time I fell out of that tree when I was a kid. This time though there was no laughter and no adrenalin. It was as if my life had been draining away. I never, ever want to feel like that again.

Chapter 32

I know you're going to want to know how much money I got for the lift but I'm afraid I can't tell you. What I will tell you is that a few months before I had a bet on myself with a famous online bookmaker. Their odds of 25/1 looked quite attractive so I decided to have a punt. Once again, I couldn't possibly tell you what the stake was but let's just say I took full advantage of the odds.

Funnily enough, about the time I put the bet on I was talking to the Lithuanian strongman, Vytautas Lalas. He'd come over to Stoke for a competition we were both appearing in and he said to me, 'Eddie, do you honestly think you can pull 500kg?'

'Seriously, Vytautas,' I said. 'I will pull that weight. I've just had a big bet on myself and if you've got any sense you'll do the same.'

'Honestly?' he said.

'Look, mate,' I said to him. 'If you put £5,000 on you'll get about £125,000 back. Trust me.'

'OK,' he said. 'I'm doing it!'

I haven't seen Vytautas since then so have no idea if he did or not. I bet he fucking didn't.

The following day was Max's fourth birthday party and I don't mind admitting that it brought me down to earth with an almighty thud. We must have had about forty people in the house that day and apart from a couple of them saying, 'Well done, Ed,' nobody said a frigging word. Yes, OK, I know it was Max's party. The night before I'd experienced the biggest high of my life and normality was difficult to deal with. In the end I asked Rich to give me a massage so while everyone was downstairs on the bouncy castle he got to work on my back. What a state that was in. Rich said it felt like two pieces of steel.

What ended up easing my transition back to normality this time around was the amount of coverage it received worldwide. To this day, I have never seen anything like it in strongman, regardless of the event, and there's been nothing like it since. Even World's Strongest Man doesn't receive this kind of exposure. As well as trending on Facebook and Twitter it even made the news on ESPN America! That might sound a bit trivial to some people but for a niche sport like strongman it's a massive achievement. A big, big thing.

Speaking of World's Strongest Man, that was my next competition. In five weeks' time!

CHAPTER 33
Two Fingers

After the lift, I stayed away from the gym for a week and instead concentrated on my recovery. The majority of these sessions were physio, hot and cold treatments, or stretching, and after every session I felt better and better. Never had I been so in need of rehabilitation and that week was just amazing. I could actually feel my body coming back to life.

By the time I went back to the gym the following Monday I had exactly four weeks to prepare for World's Strongest Man. I was over the depression now and in addition to looking forward to appearing at the World's I was able to appreciate the enormity of what I'd achieved. Obliterating the world record like that amplified my self-confidence like you wouldn't believe and as opposed to just strolling into the gym like I'd always done, I was now trotting! All I wanted to do was train, train, train, and so basically, I increased everything. I increased my training, my food, my physio and my hot and colds. I'd just become the first man ever to lift half a tonne and without wanting to sound like a bighead, although I probably will, I was the most famous strongman on the planet. If I wanted to maintain that position and do justice to the lift – and to my reputation – I had to act accordingly. Best of all, I actually *wanted* to do this. For the first time in a while I was actually enjoying being a strongman.

By the time I got on that plane to Botswana there was no doubt in my mind that I was going to win 2016 World's Strongest Man. My plan was that when I won the competition I would retire from it immediately and then consolidate my position as the best in Britain. I'd do other things too, hopefully, but when I boarded that plane in August 2016 what I thought I was doing was attending my own semi-retirement party. I had all our holidays planned and because Alex had, and has, been through so much on my behalf, I was looking forward to treating her like a queen. Best of all, we were finally going to have that honeymoon we'd never had. The excitement I felt was incredible because you know how important it is for me to follow through on my promises. This one was the biggest of them all and to be honest the ambition had been going on for quite some time. Because there was no doubt in my mind that I would win, I'm afraid I'd lulled myself into a state of blissful ignorance and if there was ever a time when I could have done with those seeds of doubt I mentioned earlier it was now. What is it they say? Be careful what you wish for? Unfortunately this had disaster written all over it.

Botswana seemed like an amazing place and I wished I'd had time to have a look around. The hotel we stayed at was by a lake that was full of crocodiles and hippos and so that was a surreal experience. Especially for somebody more used to seeing shopping trollies in shitty canals! The only thing that worried me slightly while flying in to Botswana was the temperature. The average temperature there in August is about twenty-eight degrees Centigrade, whereas in Stoke it's probably more like eight. It hadn't been a problem in Los Angeles the year before but these things can differ massively and competing in hot temperatures was just about the only thing I hadn't trained for. In the end it was fine as there was a bit of a breeze and all in all I think I do quite well in the heat.

The day before the heats began I was still walking around in fairyland. I was bigger than I'd ever been before, strong as fuck, swimming in confidence, and on the verge of achieving my dream. Then, that afternoon, I went to what's called a familiarisation session, which basically gives the athletes a chance to familiarise themselves with the equipment. The only kit I wasn't sure of was the stuff they were using in the loading event so I made a beeline for that. It was supposed to be the first event in the heats, and you had to load four barrels onto a platform for time. It's standard stuff but I wanted to make sure I knew what I was handling.

When I picked up the barrel it felt fine and so I had a quick run with it. Yep, no problems there. Then I thought, *I know, I'll just try and throw it onto my shoulder and see if that makes it easier to carry*. Don't ask me why I did this, I just did. But as I went to throw it up I heard the most horrendous crack. Everyone in the entire yard stopped what they were doing and looked. I was wearing a glove at the time and when I took it off the ring finger and the middle finger on my left hand were at least five times their usual size. Colin Bryce was with me and I just saw his jaw drop.

'Colin,' I said to him. 'I'm out. That's it. I'm out.'

After that both of us just looked at each other in a state of incredulity. What the fuck had I just done? I couldn't believe how stupid I'd been. Both my fingers had been dislocated but because it had never happened to me before I didn't have the knowhow to protect myself.

You had to grip the barrel with a flat hand and unfortunately when I tried to throw it onto my shoulder the very end of my fingers had got caught underneath the rim. The rest of my fingers were straight and so with all that stress on the tendons they just went snap.

Despite being gutted beyond belief I decided to carry on with the competition. A lot of that was down to pressure, mainly from myself. The vast majority of people in my position would have buggered off home. This was my life, though. My career. I didn't have a job to go back to like most strongmen so I had to stay put and try to make it work. There was a pride element, too. I'd never walked away from anything in my life and I wasn't going to start now. The telephone call to Alex was devastating and although she did her best to sound philosophical I could tell that she was gutted. She must have been thinking, *Oh hell. Another year of this!*

Do you know, I'm trying to put a gloss on this situation because actually, it didn't turn out too bad. That's just not good enough for me, though. Even if I hadn't got carried away with the whole retirement thing I'd still have been devastated at not being able to win. That's what hurt most, I think: competing when I knew that I couldn't win the title. It was like going for a walk around the Yorkshire Dales with a couple of electrodes strapped to your bollocks.

In my qualifying group I had Nick Best, Grzegorz Szymański and Adam Bishop, so some big strong lads. Even so, I still managed to win the group by five clear points so I went into the final with a glimmer of hope. Only a glimmer.

The day before the final took place, the organisers of World's Strongest Man asked me, Brian and Thor if we'd mind visiting a hospital to make a few speeches and hand out some prizes. Sorry, but why on earth would you ask three athletes who are about to compete in the final of a competition to visit a hospital full of sick people? Under normal circumstances I'd have been first on the bus but the way my luck was going I'd have come away with malaria or something. It didn't make any sense to me and so I'm afraid I had to decline.

The first event in the final was the frame carry and because it wasn't one of my strongest events I had trained my fucking arse off for it. I'd even brought in a grip specialist who'd visited my gym twice a week for five months and without exaggerating my grip was just phenomenal. This bloke had cost me an absolute fortune but because I needed the help, it was worth it. I also knew that the rest of the field thought I didn't stand a chance in this event so I'd been itching to prove them wrong. But that was before the accident. Now, the only thing that was itching was my arse.

When the whistle went I locked on and when I tried to pick it up both my fingers dislocated again. The pain was excruciating – like nothing I'd ever experienced – and I'm surprised I didn't faint. I knew that every other athlete would have points after this and I was buggered if I was going to be alone on zero. As long as I managed to pick it up I'd be awarded one point and so after pulling myself together and preparing for the pain, I did just that. I may have finished last, but at least I wasn't pointless.

That smidgen of hope I mentioned had evaporated by now and from here on in it was all a matter of pride. I might not have been able to win the war, but I could still come out fighting in a battle or two. The next event was the circus barbell to overhead. This was usually a good event for me but because I couldn't grip the bar properly I knew I'd have difficulty. As well as being dislocated, my fingers were ridiculously swollen, so even if I did manage to lift the barbell off the ground I'd have to put all the pressure on my right. I don't know how the fucking hell I did it but even with all that going on I still managed eight reps and ended up coming joint first with Thor. In training I'd been doing ten reps so I should have bloody won it.

Event three was deadlift for max and after everyone else had dropped out it was left to me and Brian Shaw to fight it out. This was like a dream come true for me because not only is Brian one of the greatest strongmen who's ever lived, he's also the most professional athlete I've ever come into contact with. Going toe to toe with him in the final of World's Strongest Man – a title he'd already won three times, by the way – was a big moment for me. Nobody's taught me more in the world of strongman than Brian and I'm proud to call him a friend.

As I said, his professionalism is second to none and if there's a device out there that will help improve your grip, even by 1 per cent, Brian will have it before anyone else knows it's even out there. He would spend his last dollar on becoming stronger, and his dedication to the sport, and to becoming the best ever, is forensic. I'm exactly the same in that respect but that's only because of him. I've picked things up from loads of athletes over the years but Brian's the only one I've actually imitated. Before I met him, if somebody had ever suggested that I need to spend £50 a week on physio I'd have told them to fuck off. Nobody I knew spent £50 a week on physio and even the very thought of it was just ludicrous. What Brian did was tell me *why* I should spend that kind of money and made me see it as an investment, not a cost. Only a prat would ignore his expertise. These days I spend nearly £200 a week on physio and although that's almost a wage to some people, it's a necessity to me. Even if I wasn't a pro and couldn't really afford it I'd get a paper round or something to pay for it. I might even be persuaded to sell my body! Whatever I spend,

I know I'll make it back ten-fold. That's the way you've got to look at it.

Because of where I was in the points I knew that I couldn't win the competition so I said to Brian, 'Look, rather than us both risking injury for the sake of half a point, why don't we shake hands and draw this event,' and he agreed. To me it didn't make any difference but to Brian it obviously did so he snapped my hand off. Would I have beaten him if I'd carried on? Well, of course I would. Do you know anybody on the planet who can live with me at deadlift? My mentality had changed momentarily and because I could no longer win the actual contest it was as close as I'd ever come to throwing in the towel.

The next event, which took place the following day, was the plane pull. Not the truck pull, but the plane pull! A C-130 Hercules Air Transporter, to be exact, weighing a colossal forty-five tonnes? It's not everyday you're asked to pull a plane twenty-five metres and I was looking forward to it.

This was meant to be a timed event to see who could finish the course fastest, but with nobody managing to complete the course it was all down to distance. Even though the fingers were a factor and made me drop the rope, I still managed third place behind Thor and Brian Shaw. In fact, I ended up finishing just six centimetres behind Brian.

After that event I lay fourth behind Brian, Thor and the very talented Georgian lad, Konstantine Janashia. To be honest, I couldn't believe how well I'd done, but I was still pissed off at not being able to contend.

The fifth and penultimate event was the kettlebell throw and I finished fourth, just behind Jean-François Caron. This again was affected by my fingers and at the end of each throw I was in absolute agony. It was a sadist's paradise! In training I'd done six in around fifty seconds but on this occasion I managed just five in 56.92. A good effort but not much else. I would never have beaten Brian and Thor at this event but I might just have snatched third. Shoulda woulda coulda ...

Going into the last event I was one point off third and about eight points off the lead. Bar Thor and Brian dropping down dead and leaving me their points in their wills, the best I could hope for was a podium finish – my first at World's Strongest Man. You see the efforts I'm going to to make this sound positive!

In order to secure third, I had to beat Janashia on the atlas stones and that's exactly what I did. I threw the first four up as quickly as I could and then once I saw that Janashia was struggling I put up the fifth up at my leisure.

Now then. Do I think that if I hadn't had the accident I would have won World's Strongest Man 2016? Yes, of course I do. And that's not because I'm deluded or anything. It's a simple case of mathematics. Based on what I'd done in training, if I'd been fit and Brian and Thor had finished on the same points I would have won the competition. The thing is, I didn't, did I, so basically it's a complete load of bollocks. Anything can happen during a competition and the last thing I was going to do was become obsessed with what might have happened had I not been a silly twat at the familiarisation session. Life's too fucking short for all that crap.

In all seriousness I was extremely pissed off at coming third and when I stood on the podium and looked up at Thor and Brian I thought, *What a load of absolute wank*. I should have been standing in the middle. I'd still have been smaller than Thor and Brian but at least I'd have had a bigger trophy. I'm trying to decide if I was feeling sorry for myself and to be honest I probably was. I still had that overriding desire to come first, which was obviously at odds with where I was on the podium, but I couldn't help thinking that I'd been dealt a bad hand – pardon the pun.

That evening, Brian Shaw and I went out for a meal and I remember saying to him that I should have done a lot better. What I also said is that even if I had done better, I don't think I'd have beaten him. That really wasn't like me at all. All this magnanimous bollocks had to stop!

When I arrived back in Stoke the atmosphere was flat to say the least. My usual grievances of a lack of recognition and difficulty in adjusting to normal life had been superseded by an overwhelming sense of disappointment; not just for me but for Alex too. Everything I'd sensed over the phone was true and when I saw her face for the first time it spelled just three words – *not another year*. She obviously didn't say as much but it was written all over her. I felt the same, but for slightly different reasons. For me the biggest problem, apart from not being able to keep my promise to Alex, was being so fucking heavy. Over the past twelve months or so I'd been swimming in some very dark waters and I also had to think about my future health. At six foot three inches I'm not small, but I'm nowhere near tall enough to carry thirty-one or thirty-two stone. Not on an ongoing basis and certainly not while I was putting my body under so much pressure. Because of all the swimming I've done in the past my heart is extremely healthy but by carrying so much weight I knew I was abusing that advantage daily. Sooner or later it was going to catch up with me and at the time it was starting to become a worry.

Over the next week or so, Alex and I talked a lot about the future and I managed to persuade her to give me one more year. The sacrifices she makes, not to mention the effort she puts in, are equal to mine and so I knew if it didn't happen it would be the end of us. For a start I'd be a nightmare to live with and despite all the positive aspects of our relationship, the negative ones – all the sacrifices she makes and all the promises I've failed to keep – would cast too big a shadow over our relationship. I love Alex more than anyone else on Earth but ultimately I knew that could be our downfall. Letting her down doesn't just kill her, it kills me too. The next nine months were going to be crucial.

CHAPTER 34

The Here And Now

In about a week's time I'll be flying out to Botswana for World's Strongest Man, so before I lose my temper sitting on a plane for twenty-four fucking hours I'll just bring you up to date with what's been going on and tell you about all the preparation I've been doing. As I write this chapter it's now the middle of May 2017, and I've still got everything to play for.

From a competition point of view it's been up and down and if you were basing my chances of winning World's Strongest Man on the last two competitions it would be in the balance. The first one, which took place in March 2017, was Britain's Strongest Man at the Doncaster Dome. As Britain's most prestigious strongman event this was extremely important to me and after holding the title every year since 2014 I was obviously mad keen to retain it.

Well, to say I had a good day would be an understatement, because as well as winning three of the five events I finished the competition 14.5 points ahead of second place. That's a ridiculously impressive lead and proves that I'm the best in Britain by a long, long way.

Chapter 34

On top of the prize money for the event I also won a motorbike and at the end of the competition I rode it out of the Doncaster Dome in front of the crowd, burned some rubber, and then rode back in again. Any chance to show off.

Next on the agenda was Europe's Strongest Man at Leeds Arena. That took place on April Fool's Day, and, given my performance, it was very, very apt. This was always going to be a two-way battle between me and Thor and to be honest with you, I thought I was going to whip his fucking ass. This assessment was based on how I'd improved since last year, but what it didn't consider was how Thor might also have improved. Unfortunately for me, he had, and to be honest with you, I had seriously underestimated him. Like me, he'd obviously upped his game and he's definitely stronger than last year. A lot stronger. Everybody knows what Thor is capable of and if he gets it right in training, he could be one of the best there's ever been. Although the competition was tight – just two points in the end – he was definitely the better man and I was far from being my best. Not even breaking the world axle press record, which I did towards the start of the competition, could cheer me up and all in all it was a bad day at the office.

My only excuse for delivering such a lacklustre performance, apart from some stress at home, was the heart attack I'd had about ten days before. Well, it felt like a fucking heart attack! While having my bloods done one day I was told that I was a little bit low on potassium. 'Just eat a few bananas or take a supplement for a week' was the advice I was given, and really, that should have been that.

Because it was so close to Europe's Strongest Man I'm afraid I panicked a bit and as opposed to doing what I'd been told and either taking a supplement or eating a few bananas, I took lots of supplements *and* ate mountains of lovely bananas. Little did I know that by taking in too much potassium I was in danger of giving myself a heart attack. It didn't take long for me to find out.

After I'd been popping supplements and gorging on bananas a few days I started getting cramps all over my body. My arms and legs were the worst but I even got them in my bloody eyes. Fuck, that was painful. After that I started twitching everywhere and because I thought it was all down to having low potassium I ate more bananas and popped even more pills.

A few days later, this would have been about 20 March, I got into bed about 11 p.m. and the moment I lay down, my heart started beating at about a hundred miles an hour. *That's not right,* I thought. *I'm not stressed about anything and all I'm doing is resting.* After putting a finger pulse oximeter on, it came up with a reading of 140 beats per minute. Bear in mind a normal resting heart rate is 60 to 100 beats per minute, less if you're very fit. 'I'm going to sit downstairs for a bit,' I said to Alex. 'Something's not right.'

Things like this had happened before and so I wasn't too worried. Sure enough, about ten minutes later, my heartbeat started to drop. The thing is, it didn't stop dropping and within about ten minutes it was down to 30 beats a minute. 'Alex, call an ambulance,' I said in a panic. My left arm had now started tingling and when I started getting pins and needles down it I thought I was fucked. The paramedics arrived in about five minutes flat, by which time my heartbeat had gone back up to about 120. After running some tests, they told me that my potassium levels were dangerously high and that my heart had gone into spasm. That's when I realised what had happened. *What a fucking berk,* I thought. *I've almost bloody killed myself.*

The paramedics recommended that I go into hospital for some treatment but before I agreed I asked them for a media block. I didn't want people seeing me with wires sticking out of my chest, especially so close to a competition, so before we set off they rang the hospital to see if it would be OK. 'I'll pay for the private room,' I said. 'And anything else that's necessary.'

I have no idea why, but for some unknown reason the matron or the sister or whoever said no to the media block. They had rooms, according to the paramedics, but the answer was still no. 'Well, I'm afraid I can't go in then,' I said to them. 'It'd be a nightmare.' They tried to persuade me otherwise but I was having none of it. In the end, I just sat up and flushed the potassium out by drinking gallons and gallons of water and after about seven or eight hours my heart rate started normalising again. The next day I couldn't train and it took me a good two or three days after that to feel normal again. It taught me a lesson. Just fucking listen!

Europe's Strongest Man took place about a month and a half ago now, and it's enabled me to make a few tweaks and get that little bit closer to where I need to be. Seriously, if Thor puts in a performance like that at World's Strongest Man I'm going to have a serious problem on my hands. Given how confident I usually am that may sound a bit defeatist. It's not meant to be; I know I can still beat Thor. He knows that too. The problem is, he can also beat me, so it'll all be down to who's best on the day.

That show, by the way, had an audience of over 11,000, which as far as I know is one of the largest ever in strongman. I haven't included many adverts in this book but if there's anyone reading this who has never been to a strongman event before then take my advice and go. As a form of family entertainment it's got everything and, unlike football or any of that bollocks, there are no boring bits. It's all full-on action and if you go to one that I'm involved in, all the better. Our sport is now bigger than it's ever been and if you're reading this you must at least have an interest. Seriously, if you haven't been to one before, just go. You'll absolutely love it.

You remember I mentioned the Las Vegas-style introductions at the Arnold Classic? Well, Colin Bryce is getting quite good at that and because the competitions are becoming so big we decided to make the introductions a little bit more interesting. As I'm called 'The Beast' I suggested to Colin that we should play on that a bit. 'What do you have in mind?' he said. 'How about some massive chains and a mask?' I suggested. I have no idea what Colin *thought* I was going to suggest, but one thing I do know is, it wasn't that. Fortunately he quickly warmed to the idea and a couple of days later my costume arrived. 'Now all I need is some music to go with it,' I said to him. 'You just leave that to me,' he said. The result had the audience on their feet and if you tune into the competition later in the year when it's televised you'll see exactly what Colin and I came up with. I did suggest taking the mask and chains with me to World's Strongest Man but apparently they've been confiscated. Probably a good thing.

The only scare I've had recently took place about ten days ago at the start of May, but fortunately it turned out to be blessing in disguise.

Once a year, all strongmen have to have an ECG and when I went for mine it detected what's called a suboccipital decompression, which causes heart rate variability. What the doctor couldn't understand was that my blood pressure was 120 over 60, which, for a thirty-stone man, is just ridiculous. Ridiculous in a good way, I should add. He checked it about ten times just to make sure but it still came out the same.

The results of the ECG went straight back to the governing body's medical team who told me that until the decompression had been explained I wouldn't be able to compete. They also instructed me to have an echocardiogram as soon as possible. With only three weeks to go I was terrified and instead of waiting for an appointment with the NHS, which would have taken years, I booked in with my local Nuffield hospital.

After the echocardiogram, which seemed to take an age, the doctor said I had the most efficient heart he'd ever come across and because it was so efficient even the smallest anomaly would be flagged as a problem.

'Tell the governing body that, and quick!' I asked him. 'I'm supposed to fly in a couple of weeks.'

Damaging my heart has always been a worry for me, especially since I've been this big, so receiving the news that my heart was so healthy has done me the power of good. It's like I've been given permission to push that little bit harder.

That just about brings us up to the present day. As I'm sitting here now I am genuinely more focused and positive than I have ever been in my entire life. About strongman, that is. From the moment I get up until the moment I get to bed all I can visualise is lifting that trophy. Thor and Brian are beside me, still towering over me of course, but I'm in the middle. I am the fucking winner. I've always said that unless I die or unless a doctor tells me to stop, I will become World's Strongest Man. I honestly can't remember the first time I said that, but I'll tell you one thing, I have never been so sure of it in my entire life.

I have got a lot of injuries at the moment. In fact, I'm riddled with them. The difference is between now and last year is that not one of them will affect any of the events I'll be competing in. There is a slight shoulder problem that worries me a bit but I'm confident I'll get that sorted before I go.

The events at this year's World's Strongest Man suit me down to the ground so I've never stood a better chance of winning.Three of the events should be bankers for me: the squat, the deadlift and the Viking press. If I win those three events like I should do, all I have to do is get a top three finish in the remaining three. If I do that I will be crowned 2017 World's Strongest Man. Do the other three events worry me? To be honest, they do, a little bit. But this is where those seeds of doubt I mentioned earlier come in useful. Winning the first three events might turn out to be a lot easier than coming second or third in the second three. Then again, it could be the other way around. The second three events, by the way, are the plane pull, the tyre flip and drag, and the atlas stones. In the absence of any aeroplanes in Newcastle, I've been using a lorry from that local skip company again to train that, and when it comes to the tyre I've managed to source the exact same one they'll be using in the competition. A drag's a drag, so all you need to do to train that is pick up a T-bar and drag some weight. Believe it or not I don't actually train for atlas stones. It's just a case of grunting that stone from A to B and as long as you use the right tacky, which is the stuff we put on our forearms – and, as long you're strong enough, of course – then you should be OK. There are actually all kinds of tacky, and which type you use depends on the temperature. That's why I always carry a thermometer to competitions.

The most essential thing I'll be taking with me this year to World's Strongest Man is Rich, my sports therapist. All in, that's going to cost me about six or seven grand but it's worth every single penny. A lot of people will think I'm mad for doing it but he's the best there is and so when I lift that trophy it'll be the best six or seven grand I've ever spent. At Europe's a few weeks ago, and at Britain's, I was the only strongman who brought his own physio. In fact, because it was so fast-paced at Europe's, I had two. Each was handed their own sheet of paper at the beginning of the night telling them exactly what to do and when. All I had to do was lie there and let them get on with it. There are physios available at strongman events but if they don't know your body it just doesn't work. For me, anyway. Some might call that being anal but I call it professional.

One of the many differences between this year's World's Strongest Man and earlier events is that this year every single base has been covered. There are no – repeat, no – excuses. If I get beaten at this year's competition it will be down to either strength, bad luck or injury, and I obviously can't legislate for the last two. I simply have to deliver.

It's fair to say it's become an obsession and you would not believe the lengths I've gone to. Actually, by now you probably would. I'm going to tell you anyway.

Do any of you know what hyperbaric oxygen therapy (HBOT) is? It's a medical treatment that enhances the body's natural healing process and it takes place in what's called a hyperbaric chamber. While you're in there you inhale pure oxygen and you're able to increase and control the atmospheric pressure. I usually have it at about 22psi which is about one and a half atmospheric pressures. That's the equivalent to being twenty metres under water and the atmospheric pressure forces the oxygen into your muscles and opens all your capillaries and arteries. That's a layman's description, by the way.

To put the effectiveness of the therapy into perspective, one hours' in a hyperbaric chamber is the equivalent to twelve hours' recovery time. And, the less time I need to spend recovering, the more time I can spend training. It's that simple.

A hyperbaric chamber would normally cost at least a hundred grand but it's basically a rolled piece of steel with a Perspex window in it and, because I'm quite a practical person, I decided to build my own. It's now in my gym at the bottom of my garden and it's a hell of a piece of kit. You've got to be so, so careful what you take in there (no jewellery or mobiles, etc) and to be honest it's as boring as hell. I usually do about an hour and a half a day.

Training too has gone up a gear and I've almost killed myself at least twice. I remember one instance on the leg press. I was doing over a thousand kilos and after doing eight reps all I remember is waking up with the weights about an inch from my chest. Fuck knows how I managed to extract myself, but I did. That was a scary one. I also passed out while training the log press one day and it smashed against the back of my head. How many fucks did I give? Not one.

In the powerlifting world, i.e. squat, deadlift and bench, I was doing weights that would make the best in the world look second rate. I was benching 265kg (584 lb) for six reps and the British record is only 250kg (551 lb). In the squat, I was doing 345kg (761 lb) for ten plus reps and the British record is 380kg (838 ln). But that's only one rep. The deadlift speaks for itself but the person closest to me in Britain is Loz Shahlaei on 435kg (959 lb). That's a 65kg difference! That's how strong I had to be.

After I'd built the hyperbaric chamber and had bought myself new hot and cold tubs, which again are essential for recovery, I was on the verge of being skint. If Alex had known how bad things were, she'd have gone apeshit. I had to do it though. Everything I have, financially, physically and mentally, has gone into winning this competition. I think I'd sell my house if I'd needed to. I've definitely sold my soul.

NO – FUCKING – EXCUSES.

I'll tell you what. Let me just take you through a typical day in the run up to this competition. You honestly won't believe it.

2 a.m. – Get up. Eat some steak and drink a litre of protein shake.

7 a.m. – Get up and have another protein shake. This time with spinach, ice cream, nuts, butter, protein powders, raspberries and blueberries.

9 a.m. – Get up and have a full English breakfast. Five or six of everything. Wash it down with a litre of cranberry juice.

9.45 a.m. – Go out for a brisk walk.

10 a.m. – Eat 100g cashew nuts and drink half a litre of protein shake.

10.15 a.m. – Back to bed. Because I'm in training I'll be knackered so I won't just lie there. I'll be fast asleep.

12.30 p.m. – Get up and start cooking dinner which will either be spaghetti bolognaise or chicken, rice and pasta. I'll also have half a large cheesecake for pudding and a litre of cranberry juice. That meal alone will be at least 3,500 calories.

1.30 p.m. – Back to sleep.

3.10 p.m. – Get up, pack for the gym and start eating again. Tuna sandwich, flapjack, bananas, beef jerky and two large bottles of Lucozade.

3.30 p.m. – Set off to the gym and carry on eating. Flapjacks, nuts and bananas.

3.45 p.m. – Start training my fucking arse off. No time limit. I train until I drop and if I don't pass out I will definitely vomit at some point during the session. It's as simple as that. Everything's become so extreme. All the way through I'm eating things like steak and beef jerky and I'll drink at least three litres of cranberry juice. How I don't actually look like a fucking cranberry I have no idea.

8 p.m. – At the end of the session I'll drink a litre of full fat milk with two scoops of protein powder. Then, I'll drink a litre of coconut water.

8.15 p.m. – Drive straight to M-Club and stretch off for half an hour. Every muscle group. After that I'll alternate between the sauna and the cold tub.

9.30 p.m. – Back home for tea. Steak, chicken, pasta, curry. Something like that. Then I'll have the other half of the cheesecake. That'll be at least another 3,000 calories.

10.15 p.m. – Alex will go to bed and I'll go to the hyperbaric chamber for ninety minutes. Because of the noise it's impossible to fall asleep so I just lie there in the dark.

11.45 p.m. – Have a quick snack, something like a protein bar, then try and get some sleep before I'm up again.

There. Not exactly a ride on the big dipper, is it? This has been my life every day now for the last six months and as extreme as it might seem I've actually become used to it. Eating to the point of vomiting is the bit I dislike the most and once I've finally won this competition I'll definitely cut back.

She's given me permission to say this, but the only thing that's been really difficult over the last six months has been my relationship with Alex. Since coming back from World's Strongest Man 2016 it's been on a downward spiral and given what I've already told you it's not difficult to see why. As well as holding a job down she's had to do everything; clean the house, take Max to school, do the shopping – the lot. Worst of all she's had a husband who may as well have been on another planet. The only time I spend with her and the kids is a couple of hours on a Saturday but because I'm knackered I can't go anywhere. To be honest it's been making her ill, but what can I do? I can't give up now. I've come too far. I keep saying to her, 'It's only a few more weeks. After that, I promise things will change.' I don't think she listens to me anymore. Who can blame her?

Quite a few people – very daring people – have been asking me what I'll do if I don't win this year's competition and I haven't been able to answer. All I know is that I stand to lose everything, and when I say everything, I obviously don't mean my house and my fucking car. I mean my family. The only thing I can liken it to is when a soldier leaves the army. You hear all kinds of horror stories about those poor men and women not being able to adjust and that's exactly what I'm scared of. The only difference between me and them is that if it goes tits up for me it will be all my own fault.

The thing that a lot of people have trouble understanding, and I'm one of them, is the self-destructive nature of what I do. I mean, come on. Why would anyone subject their bodies, and their minds, to such ridiculous amounts of punishment, while at the same time alienating their family? It's actually quite irrational when you think about it, but then that's strongman. Apart from wanting to lift more weight than the next man, nothing really makes sense.

I said in the documentary that the only reason I was doing this was for Alex and the kids, but am I? Am I really? Do I want to make them proud or do I want to be the centre of attention? If I'm being brutally honest I'd say both. The difference is that I might actually be able to live without being the centre of attention. What I can't live without is my family.

What gives me hope is that my desire to be congratulated is part nature, part nurture. I've always been a show-off, as you know, and from the moment I stepped onto the blocks at my first swimming gala I've been trying to wrap myself in layer after layer of acknowledgement and approval. That, my friends, is my one and only addiction, and providing I can handle losing some of it, then Alex and I might, just might, be OK.

But I'm not going to lose though, am I?

Anyway, I'll see you all in Botswana.

CHAPTER 35
Botswana Diary

Thursday 18 May 2017

You remember I mentioned not being able to legislate for luck or injury? Well, fortunately I haven't been injured yet, but if my luck carries on like this it won't be long before I am. I've been in Botswana for a day now and everything that could have gone wrong, has.

Let's start with the journey, shall we? We didn't fly until about 7 p.m. and so I spent the first half of the day packing, eating, stretching and having a bit of physio. At about 4 p.m. we set off to the airport and from the moment we arrived there everything seemed to go wrong.

For once, I'd actually paid to go in the priority lanes at security yet everyone who wasn't in the priority lanes seemed to get through before me. It's a good job I didn't swear at anybody because this time they'd probably have given me a full cavity body search!

After posing for about a hundred photographs, which I didn't mind, I made my way to the business class lounge where I was hoping to have a meal. Business class? This was more like dog class. The food there was absolutely disgusting and so because of that I ended up missing a meal. I'm not the fussiest eater in the world but this was beyond the pale. *No matter,* I thought. *There'll be plenty of food on the planes.*

We were catching three flights in all – Manchester to Paris, Paris to Johannesburg, and Johannesburg to Gaborone, which is the capital of Botswana. The first flight went fine, although there was no food. *Never mind,* I thought. *The next flight is where business class kicks in, so not long to wait.*

After going through security for a second time and then posing for another twenty photographs, I finally made my way to the gate for the flight to Johannesburg. The plane was a 747. As I boarded I handed the steward my ticket and he very kindly said he'd show me to my seat, which, according to him, was right at the front of the plane. As he led on, I quickly realised that he was taking me into economy class instead by mistake but by the time I managed to attract his attention it was too late.

'Oh, I'm so sorry, sir,' he said. 'You're obviously supposed to be in business class.'

'Yes, I know I am,' I replied through gritted teeth.

'Well,' said the steward. 'I'm afraid it's quite a journey. You need to go right to the back of the plane, up the stairs, and walk back to the very front of the plane. Your seat is directly above us.'

What an absolute fucking dickhead.

Because all the passengers were trying to put their hand luggage into the overhead lockers it took me thirty-five minutes to get from there to my seat and I ended up being the very last person to sit down. I was first on, for fuck's sake!

One of the most important things I take with me on a night flight is my sleep apnea machine, as if I fall asleep without it I can actually die. Even if I'm not planning on going to sleep I can still drop off and so unless I'm eating I have to wear it. Anyway, as I started to unpack my stuff I quickly realised that I didn't have the mask for my machine, which meant I couldn't use it. I must have lost it going through security or something but without it I couldn't fly.

'Excuse me,' I said to one of the stewards. 'I've left my sleep apnea mask in security, and without it I can't fly.'

'What do you mean, you can't fly?' This one was a bit of a grumpy twat.

'I mean, that if I fly without it, I could die.'

'Well,' he said. 'What do you want us to do about it?' Fuck knows what they were like in economy. They probably carried tasers or something.

'I've got a spare one in my luggage, but that's obviously in the hold. Somebody's going to have to get it, I'm afraid.'

'Oh, no, no, no,' he said. 'I'm afraid that's impossible.'

'Well, I can't fly without it, and I'm certainly not getting off. It's up to you. I'll just stay standing here until it arrives.'

Fortunately the captain agreed to them finding it but because it took about twenty-five minutes we ended up missing our slot. We obviously took off but thanks to me we were almost an hour late. Three hundred and sixty people all delayed by a thirty-one-stone strongman with a potentially deadly sleep disorder. You couldn't make it up.

By the time they found the mask I'd become so worked up that I was on the brink of collapsing and I was pouring with bloody sweat. For some reason the air conditioning wasn't working and unfortunately they couldn't fix it, which meant I just carried on sweating. World's Strongest Man was going to be a walk in the fucking park compared to this.

Once we were finally in the air I took a couple of painkillers, put my mask on, and tried to get some sleep, but because it was so hot I found it impossible. I'd have stripped off but all I was wearing was a pair of shorts and a vest.

To make matters worse, the bloke who was sitting next to me had a really bad cold and so as well as preventing me from resting with all his coughing and spluttering, he was also putting me at risk of getting ill. Once again the food was shit and so that was now three meals I'd missed. Thank fuck I'd packed plenty of snacks.

After pissing about in Johannesburg for a couple of hours, I found out that Rich, my physio, had been put on a later flight to Gaborone. So, as I was driving us both to the hotel, I'd have to wait for him. Ninety fucking minutes I was sitting there, and that was after I'd been to sort out the hire car.

Chapter 35

By this point I don't think I'd ever been as stressed in my entire life. I'm surprised I haven't needed fucking therapy! Perhaps I do?

By the time we eventually got to the hotel all the other athletes had checked in, eaten, bought a load of Gatorade and were relaxing in the pool. I, on the other hand, was standing there in reception feeling like a slightly malnourished gorilla who'd been locked in a fucking sauna for twenty-four hours and had his bananas pinched.

After unpacking and having a shower, I went to the shop, bought a shedload of Gatorade, necked that, and then went to have a meal in the athletes' tent. I think I said earlier in the book that conditions for the athletes at World's Strongest Man had improved in recent years. Well, I'm afraid I have no choice than to take that back. Or at least some of it. The food in that tent was absolutely vile and I wouldn't feed it to my dog. I have got a dog, by the way. It's a Labrador pup called Jack. Anyway, for as long as I'm here I'm going to be eating out.

There's only been one problem with regards to the competition so far, but potentially it's a big one. I bumped into Colin Bryce soon after arriving and he was standing with a man from Scania. They're providing the tyres for the flip and drag event in the final and after showing me a photo of the tyres we're going to be using I've realised that I've been training with the wrong one. Fuck knows how it's happened but the one I've been using has a different tread *and* it's about 80kg

(176 lb) lighter. Nothing I can do about it now. Because of all the stress, not to mention the tyre fiasco and being fed dog food, I've kind of lost my appetite, which isn't good. What a twenty-four hours it's been. We've got the medicals tomorrow, and then the media. Time to get some rest.

Saturday 20 May 2017

Well, that was fucking fun. After a good night's kip I had some physio before making my way down for the medicals and the media. Despite us all being given a schedule for both, most of the athletes just seemed to roll up when it suited them. Like a dickhead I decided to do the same but I got there just as it was starting to piss them off. 'Go away, look at your schedule, and come back at your allotted time,' was the advice they gave me. Fair enough!

In between the medical and the media I went to the familiarisation yard, which was all fine. Apart from the tyre everything's OK and after coming out of there I could feel my appetite coming back, thank God. I've eaten jack shit in the last couple of days, compared to what I should be eating, and have got some serious catching up to do.

My favourite part of the day was the media. Sometimes I can be quite humble in an interview but this time I came out all guns blazing and was as cocky as fuck in all of them. The first question they all asked me was, 'How do you think you're going to do, Eddie?' And I gave every single one exactly the same answer, which was, 'I've already won, mate.' These people all thought I was joking and after asking for a serious answer they got the same one back. 'I'll tell you again. I've already won this.'

The reason I made that claim wasn't just because I thought it was true. It was because I wanted it to get into the heads of the other athletes and so by making such an outrageous statement I knew that the media would ask them about it. 'Eddie Hall says he's already won the title. What do you think about that?' I'm just an evil fucking genius.

The only other athlete who has scared me so far is Brian. Thor looks fit and so does Žydrūnas, but Brian looks immense. Stupidly, I went and asked him how much he weighs and at the moment he's just over thirty-three stone. Two hundred and ten fucking kilograms! I think Thor's the same as me, about thirty-one, so there isn't much in it.

There's something different about Thor. I know the competition hasn't started yet but he just doesn't seem as confident as he usually is. Perhaps it's just nerves?

Funnily enough I've been watching some videos of Thor training the events for this year's competition and he's looked absolutely fucking colossal especially in the deadlift, the squat and the overhead.

Sunday 21 May 2017

I've spent most of today trying to fuck with Brian Shaw's head. Not in a bad way. I've just been trying to wind him up a bit and plant a few seeds. I'd do the same to Thor if I could get anywhere near him, but he's got an entourage of about thirty people. He's like Leonardo Di fucking Caprio.

The task of trying to emasculate or intimidate somebody as big and powerful as Brian isn't easy, but I've had a lot of fun trying. First of all I started asking him what he thought of the events, but in a really cocky manner. 'How do you think you'll do in the squat, Brian?' I asked him. 'Not your strongest event, is it? And how about the deadlift? That's probably one of my best at the moment. I should piss that.'

After giving him some massive man slaps on the back I started saying, 'Do you know what, Brian. I reckon I'm going to win this year. In fact, I think I'm going to piss it. How do you think you're going to do, Brian? Confident? You must think you have a chance.' My campaign was absolutely relentless and in the end, I even cupcaked him. Cupcaking Brian Shaw, though! You've got to be fucking brave to do that. Brave or stupid. I think I'm probably both.

The thing is, the more I tried winding Brian up the less he reacted, and the less he reacted the more I knew I was getting to him. If people react, they're on the same page as you are, but if they don't, that page has been turned. Will definitely try it again.

Actually, while we're on the subject of winding up the competition, I can tell you that one of the biggest and funniest paradoxes within strongman is the fact that, despite us all being giants who do manly things and shout 'AAAAARGH!' a lot, it's actually one of the bitchiest sports on the planet. Because it's so niche there aren't that many athletes and because we spend so much time together, everybody's connected via Facebook. It's like living in a village, I suppose, but with that comes a bit of a village mentality. Everybody knows what everyone else is either thinking or doing and so sometimes it gets a bit daft.

A strongman would never slag off another strongman to his face, by the way. Heck no. What they do instead is get a friend of theirs to post something derogatory and then hope it gets back to the person for whom it's intended, which it usually does. It's like Chinese whispers really, and a lot of it has to do with either jealousy or fear.

Take this competition, for instance. I've heard that some people think the events have been chosen to suit me and one or two have even been complaining that it's a fix. What an absolute load of bollocks. For years now, many of the events have favoured taller athletes. For instance, keg toss, power stairs, and atlas stones on six-foot plinths. Nobody ever said a thing about them favouring taller athletes, or if they did, I never heard them. Remember what I said about fear and jealousy? They know that I'm the real deal and because they're scared of what I can achieve – and, let's face it, they have good reason to be – they're already looking for excuses. I suppose it is the ultimate compliment in a way but boy does it get on my tits. The problem is that nobody will ever come out and say something to my face whereas that's the only way I can communicate. If I've got a problem with somebody I'll tell them, and if I think something's unfair, I'll tell the powers that be. If you want to make an omelette you've got to break some eggs and if people can't handle that then tough.

Monday 22 May 2017

First day of the heats today and it started off with a fucking disaster. The event was the load and drag, and for some reason the lane I was in was a lot grittier than others and I ended up finishing fourth. This isn't an excuse, by the way, as every person who used that lane did poorly.

I've had loads of people messaging me and asking how I've done but I can't bring myself to tell them. The expectation is starting to become overwhelming. It's my own fault, I suppose. After all, I create the hype. That's the easy bit though. Anyway, tomorrow's another day.

Tuesday 23 May 2017

Normal service has resumed, thank fuck!

Today was the log press and the only man in my group who came anywhere near me was the Polish lad, Mateusz Kieliszkowski. He and I competed alongside each other and after knocking out five reps very quickly I stood back and waited for him to catch up. Once he got five I lifted a sixth and once he got six I lifted a seventh. It was all about conserving energy for me. We ran out of time in the end and finished on seven each. Should have been watching the clock.

Next up was the bus pull and as well as winning my group I also finished faster than all the other athletes, including Thor. This is normally one of his best events and beating him has really boosted my confidence. Especially as that's one of the three other events I didn't think I could win. As importantly, it will have planted a seed in Thor's head and I know for a fact he'll be fucked off. The question is, how will he respond? If he lets it get to him he'll capitulate, but the chances are he'll come out fighting. Unfortunately, they're going to be swapping the bus for a fucking plane in the final, but the main thing is he's beatable. I know it, and so does he.

I spoke to Alex earlier and told her about yesterday. I was hesitant at first because I didn't want to make her nervous but the results today seemed to reassure her. And me, as it goes. She's worried though, I can tell. Really worried. I reiterated my promise to her but I'm starting to get the feeling that she's fed up with hearing it. I obviously can't blame her for that but until I produce the goods it's all I have to offer. What also frustrates her is being stuck at home while I'm competing abroad, and that's another thing that will change once I've won. Just so long as she doesn't cheer me on or start shouting advice. Fuck no.

Wednesday 24 May 2017

Deadlift day!

What a result. Not one person in my group could deadlift and so I won the event with just four reps. Kieliszkowski, who came second, did three in about fifty seconds and I pulled my four in just under ten. Every other group winner had to pull about eight or nine which means they've all had to expend twice as much energy.

Next up was the gold bullion toss (similar to the keg toss) and I only had to throw three to win the group. Best of all, whoever was winning the groups going into the last event didn't have to take part, which means I got to conserve even more energy. That said, so did the other winners.

It's hard not to get carried away by this but I've got such a good feeling about the final; if I can get past the worry, that is. As I said, as long as I win the deadlift, the squat and the Viking press, I know I'll be home and dry. OK, maybe I should rephrase that. I *hope* I'll be home and dry.

The only other people I've been watching so far have been Brian and Thor and from what I've seen so far, Brian poses the bigger threat. As well as being enormous he definitely looks more comfortable. We'll see.

Saturday 27 May 2017

Something funny happened first thing this morning. I got shat on by a bird! I was out having a stroll and all of a sudden some landed on my arm. Not much, but enough to make me call after the perpetrator! At first, I was mildly horrified but then it reminded me of something.

Back in 2014 I was competing in Malaysia in a round of the Strongman Champion's League. Me and Thor had been swapping first and second place all the way through and after the final event we were tied on points. In this situation, you go on what's called countback, which is who had the best positions overall. Unfortunately for me, in one of the events he'd been third and I'd been fourth so he beat me by one placing.

A few days before that we'd all been to an exotic bird park and half way through the day one of them had shat down Thor's back. Everybody pissed themselves, naturally, but after the event had finished he came up to me and said, 'When that bird shat on me, I knew it was for a reason.' 'Really?' I said. 'You're putting the win down to bird shit?'

I have to admit I was confused at the time but after getting shat on this morning maybe there's something in it? I'll try anything.

It's about two hours before the first event of the final and over the last two and a half days I've done nothing but eat, stretch, hydrate, have physio and relax. I did have a problem with sciatica a few days ago and once I realised it was my mattress I went out and bought a better one. Everything's so cheap here and, sure enough, I was fine the next morning. Brian Shaw was complaining of a similar problem and once I told him what I'd done he went out and did the same. I could have stayed quiet I suppose and let him suffer, but I'm not completely evil.

I also had a bit of a problem with stiff hips yesterday, which was down to having a tight quad. This produced a brief, but nevertheless serious scare, as when I was in my room with my leg on a chair trying to stretch the quad I suddenly heard, and felt, an almighty snap. For a second I thought I might have done myself some damage but instead it fixed the problem. It was painful – snapping a quad usually is – but my movement has improved ten-fold.

Well, that's what I've been doing physically. Mentally, I've been going off my box with worry and my head's been like a hamster's wheel. The closer the final gets the more in touch I become with the rest of my life and I'd be surprised if there's a single worst-case scenario I haven't thought of yet. In terms of severity they normally range from grave to catastrophic, and unfortunately this destructive train of thought has kept me from sleeping. I even had to call out the doctor the other day and get him to prescribe me some diazepam. I only took the diazepam last night and fortunately it gave me the best night's sleep ever. I'm still worrying my fucking arse off, but at least I can do it with my eyes open today. My confidence and strength are still there, bubbling away underneath, but all I can actually *feel* is fear. Over the next two days I will have six opportunities to save the rest of my life. That may sound a bit overdramatic but that's what my head is telling me. Six events that will define my future.

Right. I've got to be down in reception in a bit so I'd better get my shit together. Wish me luck.

Sunday 28 May 2017 – COMPETITION FINISHED

I've managed to escape the press for a few minutes but have been told by the organisers that I'm not allowed to give details of what has just happened. The competition isn't televised until Christmas and obviously they want as many people to tune in as possible. That's fair enough. One thing I am allowed to do is give you an indication of who won the competition, and in order to do that I will write just four words:

I kept my promise.

Acknowledgements

As far as I know I'm one of the first strongmen to write an autobiography so it only makes sense that I thank those responsible first. They are, James Hogg, who helped me write the book. My publisher, Lorna Russell at Virgin Books, and my literary agent, Tim Bates. Thanks guys. It's been a great experience.

Next, I'd like to say a special thank you to three people who made a big difference in my early life. They are: Vivienne Mills, my first and favourite teacher – and, my first sponsor! Arnold Faulkner, my swimming coach and the man who taught me how to become a champion. And Greg Clarke, my second swimming coach and the man who taught me how to enjoy the fruits of my labours. I know I wasn't the easiest pupil so thanks for your perseverance.

I dread to think how long I've spent in the gym over the years and if it wasn't for these three lads it would have been a lot less enjoyable. They are Andy Parker at Strength Asylum, Bazza Bailey at Ultimate Fitness, and last but not least, my long-suffering training partner, Luke Fullbrook. Thanks lads.

A few years ago, I was approached by a very confident TV presenter called Matt Bell who wanted to make a documentary on my life. The resulting film, *Eddie: Strongman*, is something I'm very proud of and I'm pleased to say he's become a good friend. Well done mate and here's to the sequel!

If it hadn't been for my manager, Mo Chaudry, I wouldn't be where I am today. It's as simple as that. He was the one who made it possible for me to go full-time and all in all I think things have gone reasonably well. Mo, I will always be very, very grateful.

These days an athlete is nothing without his sponsors and it's a department in which I have been blessed. In no particular order, I'd like to thank Phil Blakeman at Blakeman's; Chris and Dave Johnson at the Pulse Group; Chris Butler; Wayne Walker at Wayne Walker Meats; Uchit Vadher at Xplosive Ape; Peter Wright at Wright's Pies; Ray, James and John at Jumbo Skips; and everyone at Protein Dynamix, MUHDO and Alpha Bottle. Thank you all for your support.

Before I move on to my family I'd just like to say thank you to the boys and girls at Giants Live – in particular Darren Sadler and Colin Bryce – and also to my good friend Neil Pickup. I'm lucky to have such good friends within the sport I love.

Over the years I've tested the patience of every member of my immediate family and in a variety of different ways. I'm anything but predictable!

Luckily for me each and every one of them has stuck with me through thick and thin, and because of that I worship the ground they walk on. They are: my brothers James and Alex, my children Layla and Maximus, my Mum and Dad, Helen and Stephen, and my wife Alex. Seriously. Words cannot express my admiration.

This book is in memory of Sheila Jackson, David Jackson and Reginald Hall.

Eddie Hall's Competition Record

Amateur competitions

2007 Burnley Novice Strongman	5th
2008 Blackburn Novice Strongman	7th
2009 Staffordshire's Strongest Man	3rd
2009 North UK's Strongest Man	7th
2010 North UK's Strongest Man	2nd
2011 NEC Birmingham Strongest Man	2nd

Britain's Strongest Man

2014 Britain's Strongest Man	1st
2015 Britain's Strongest Man	1st
2016 Britain's Strongest Man	1st
2017 Britain's Strongest Man	1st

England's Strongest Man

2010 England's Strongest Man (Elite)	1st
2011 England's Strongest Man (UKSC)	1st

Europe's Strongest Man

2012 Europe's Strongest Man	8th
2017 Europe's Strongest Man	2nd

Giants Live

Giants Live 2012 (Australia)	4th
Giants Live 2013 (Hungary)	2nd
Giants Live 2014 (Hungary)	3rd

UK's Strongest Man

2011 UK's Strongest Man	1st
2012 UK's Strongest Man	1st
2013 UK's Strongest Man	1st
2014 UK's Strongest Man	1st
2015 UK's Strongest Man	1st
2016 UK's Strongest Man	1st

World's Strongest Man

2012 World's Strongest Man	Qualified
2013 World's Strongest Man	Qualified
2014 World's Strongest Man	6th
2015 World's Strongest Man	4th
2016 World's Strongest Man	3rd
2017 World's Strongest Man	1st

Index

EH indicates Eddie Hall.

Index